BASHER
FIVE-TWO

BASHER
FIVE-TWO

THE TRUE STORY OF F-16 FIGHTER PILOT CAPTAIN SCOTT O'GRADY

CAPTAIN SCOTT O'GRADY
WITH MICHAEL FRENCH

A YEARLING BOOK

Published by
Bantam Doubleday Dell Books for Young Readers
a division of
Bantam Doubleday Dell Publishing Group, Inc.
1540 Broadway
New York, New York 10036

Visit us on the Web! www.bdd.com

Educators and librarians, visit the BDD Teacher's
Resource Center at www.bdd.com/teachers

ISBN: 0-440-41313-3

Reprinted by arrangement with Doubleday Books for Young Readers

Printed in the United States of America

August 1998

10 9 8 7 6 5 4

CWO

To all those who were part of my rescue,
and to the POWs
and MIAs, past and present, who gave me the
inspiration to survive

U.S. MILITARY CODE OF CONDUCT

I   I am an American, fighting in the forces which guard my country and our way of life. I am prepared to give my life in their defense.

II   I will never surrender of my own free will. If in command, I will never surrender the members of my command while they still have the means to resist.

III   If I am captured I will continue to resist by all means available. I will make every effort to escape and aid others to escape. I will accept neither parole nor special favors from the enemy.

IV   If I become a prisoner of war, I will keep faith with my fellow prisoners. I will give no information or take part in any action which might be harmful to my comrades. If I am senior, I will take command. If not, I will obey the lawful orders of those appointed over me and will back them up in every way.

V   When questioned, should I become a prisoner of war, I am required to give name, rank, service number, and date of birth. I will evade answering further questions to the utmost of my ability. I will make no oral or written statements disloyal to my country and its allies or harmful to their cause.

VI   I will never forget that I am an American, fighting for freedom, responsible for my actions, and dedicated to the principles which made my country free. I will trust in my God and in the United States of America.

HIGH FLIGHT

by John Gillespie Magee, Jr.

Oh, I have slipped the surly bonds of earth
  And danced the skies on laughter-silvered wings;
Sunward I've climbed, and joined the tumbling mirth
  Of sun-split clouds—and done a hundred things
You have not dreamed of—wheeled and soared and
    swung
  High in the sunlit silence. Hov'ring there,
I've chased the shouting wind along, and flung
  My eager craft through footless halls of air.
Up, up the long, delirious, burning blue
  I've topped the windswept heights with easy grace,
Where never lark, or even eagle flew.
  And, while with silent, lifting mind I've trod
The high untrespassed sanctity of space,
  Put out my hand, and touched the face of God.

ONE

In the early afternoon of June 2, 1995, as I sat in my F-16, ready for takeoff from Aviano Air Base in northeastern Italy, I had no idea what fate had in store for me. I could never have imagined that in the next six days I would have my plane shot out from under me with a missile, run for my life as soldiers hunted me down, eat leaves and ants to survive, make friends with a couple of cows, and be rescued by the United States Marines. And that was only part of my ordeal. Afterward I would call it the adventure of a lifetime. Maybe that's an understatement. It was the adventure of two lifetimes.

That summer, as a United States Air Force captain, I was one of thirty-five American pilots assigned to the 555th Fighter Squadron, or the "Triple Nickel," of the Thirty-first Fighter Wing. Our uniforms boasted a Velcro patch of a fierce bald eagle, the insignia of the Triple Nickel, and another patch showing a winged dragon, to identify the Thirty-first Fighter Wing. We were stationed in Italy as part of a North Atlantic Treaty Organization (NATO) air team. To the east of Italy, across the Adriatic Sea, was Bosnia and Herzegovina, part of the Balkans and a country in the midst of a painful civil war.

Our NATO special mission—called Operation Deny Flight—was to try to help end that war.

The Triple Nickel took turns with other NATO pilots—Dutch, Italians, French, and British—in patrolling the skies over Bosnia. Our job was to keep all military aircraft of the fighting factions—the Serbs, the Muslims, and the Croatians—out of the skies so that they couldn't hurt each other with air strikes. We were not there to take sides, but if necessary, we were to use our weapons to enforce this "no-fly zone." Neither the Serbs, the Muslims, nor the Croatians wanted us there. They would just as soon have shot *us* out of the air so that they could fight their own war. But NATO had decided we were needed, and all of us in the Triple Nickel took our duty seriously.

That morning of June 2, I showered, shaved, and laid out my olive green flight suit. My spirits couldn't have been better. Not only did I love flying an F-16, I had lucked out by being stationed in Italy with the Triple Nickel. In my six years in the U.S. Air Force, I had called nine different places home, but no location had been quite as beautiful as northeastern Italy. My apartment was in a quaint village called Montereale Val Cellina. Besides being close to the air base, I was thirty minutes from the beach in one direction and ten minutes from the Italian Alps in another. The locals were friendly, the cafés didn't serve a bad meal, and my landlords took me in as part of their family.

I slipped into my one-piece flight suit, zipping it from crotch to neck, and grabbed my logbook and wallet. Because my fridge was basically empty, I decided to skip breakfast. Climbing into my Toyota 4Runner, I left for the Aviano Air Base. I didn't *have* to fly today, but an opening in the flight schedule had come up the day before, and I had a good reason for grabbing it. Too busy with duties on the ground, I hadn't flown a mission in more than ten days. And I was due shortly to start my vacation, meeting my mom, Mary Lou Scardapane, and her husband, Joseph, to travel through Italy. It had been a long time since I'd been in the air, and an F-16 pilot never wants to get rusty.

I took my time driving to the air base. Over the years I'd become a careful driver, but my early experiences behind the wheel were no shining example for a driver's ed class. I spent my teenage years in Spokane, Washington, the oldest of three children. One thing my brother, Paul, and I had in common was a love of speed. Starting with my parents' Chevy Suburban, which I drove off an icy mountain road one afternoon and crashed into a tree, I had had a series of mostly minor car accidents in fourteen years of driving.

The worst had just happened this fall, on the same road to the Aviano base. While stationed in Germany, I had bought a BMW—it took all my money and was the first new car I'd ever owned. Of course, I'd brought it to Italy when I was transferred to Aviano. While driving around a curve in the predawn darkness, blinded by the headlights of an oncoming car, I jerked my BMW off the road. I ended up in a ditch, upside down. Fortunately, the air bag inflated, saving me from head injuries, and my fastened seat belt kept me from flying out of the car.

Although the BMW was totaled, I crawled out with barely a scratch. I had this lifelong habit of inflicting serious damage on cars, but somehow I also had the luck to escape harm to myself and others. My family, particularly my father, liked to say I had nine lives, like a cat. After the BMW disaster, it was also understood that I had better change my ways—otherwise I might go through those nine lives too quickly. That was when I bought the 4Runner and began taking those curves more slowly.

Entering the main gate of the Aviano Air Base, I passed through several security checkpoints, parked at the squadron building, and signed in at the operations, or "ops," desk to be briefed about the day's flight. From Aviano, we usually flew our sorties—air missions—over Bosnia in pairs but sometimes flew in a formation of four. Today I would be flying the more standard "two-ship" formation, with Bob Wright as the lead pilot. I would be his wingman. I was qualified to fly lead and often did, but on any given sortie you can only play one role, and today's assignment listed me as a wingman.

This would be my forty-seventh sortie over Bosnia. My call sign, or "handle," for the day's mission was Basher Five-Two. Bob, in the lead plane, would be Basher Five-One.

Bob's nickname was Wilbur—after one of the famous Wright brothers, who flew the first airplane at Kitty Hawk, North Carolina. Bob was a good friend. We had met three years earlier when we were both F-16 pilots at the Kunsan Air Base in South Korea. At thirty-three, Wilbur was still younger than a lot of F-16 pilots, but he was one of the most experienced and capable leaders I knew. Unlike the character Tom Cruise played in *Top Gun*, Wilbur, like every other F-16 pilot with whom I'd had the privilege of flying, was cool, calm, and collected. We were no reckless hotshots. The years of training to qualify to fly an F-16, and the $20 million price tag of each plane, left all pilots with a feeling of enormous responsibility. When we were flying, it wasn't like driving a car. Sure, there was the element of speed. If I maxed out, I could travel at more than twice the speed of sound. But the F-16 was so complex that it demanded an encyclopedia's worth of knowledge, split-second reflexes, and absolute, total attention every moment you were airborne. There was always a low level of fear when you were flying, but having Wilbur alongside me took off some of that edge.

We dressed for our mission in a locker room of the

squadron building. First we removed the Velcro insignia patches of the winged dragon and bald eagle from our flight suits. If we were captured, we didn't want the enemy to know the names of our units. According to a famous international treaty called the Geneva Convention, which all nations are supposed to honor, in time of war you don't have to tell the enemy anything more than your name, date of birth, rank, and serial number. Article Five of the U.S. Military Code of Conduct contains the same rule. Both Article Five and the Geneva Convention are supposed to help prevent the abuse of anyone who is captured. Of course, we all knew that in the history of war, nations had often violated such rules, sometimes using torture to extract information.

For anyone serving in the military, particularly as a fighter pilot, the risk of being captured was always a reality, but it wasn't something my fellow pilots and I dwelled on. In the several years that NATO had been flying sorties over Bosnia, only one pilot, a British captain in a Harrier jump jet, had been shot down. He had parachuted safely into Muslim territory, been captured without a struggle, and been returned by the Muslims to NATO forces the next day. I didn't think there was too much to worry about. On the other hand, I knew from our intelligence, or "intel," officer that things had been heating up. Intel officers had special information about the enemy that could help a pilot in the sky. We had been told that NATO planes had recently destroyed one of the Bosnian Serbs' weapons piles. In revenge, the Serbs had rounded up 350 unarmed NATO military observers throughout the country and made them hostages. The Serbs had physically tied the captured men to their other weapons depots, daring NATO planes to attack again.

In Bosnia, you could never be sure what would happen next. But you knew all the three factions in the civil war could be ruthless.

After removing my insignia patches, I squirmed into my G suit. This was a special tight-fitting brace or girdle that I wore over my flight suit. It wrapped around my stomach and my legs. The purpose of the G suit was to help me resist the forces of gravity—what pilots call G forces. On earth, normal gravity is one G. On a roller coaster, on a steep plunge, it's possible to feel three Gs. In an F-16, the rapid acceleration and sharp turns a pilot go through can mean pressure up to nine Gs. If someone weighs 100 pounds normally, with the pressure of 9 Gs it's as if he weighed 900 pounds. That much pressure naturally causes blood to flow from the head into the rest of the body. When that happens, a pilot can easily black out and have a fatal accident. The tight fit of the G suit, however, makes it harder for the blood to leave your head and flow into your stomach and legs. In addition, as a pilot you are taught to strain or contract your leg and stomach muscles when going into steep turns—extra insurance against blacking out.

I dropped my Swiss Army knife into a chest pocket and put on my survival vest, which included a two-way radio. I holstered my 9-mm semiautomatic Beretta pistol under my armpit and tucked my Global Positioning Satellite (GPS) receiver into another pocket. Into my G suit's right shin pocket I shoved an evasion map and a "blood chit." This was a note from the U.S. government, printed in eleven languages, including Serbian and Serbo-Croatian, that promised to pay money to anyone who hid me from the enemy.

I buckled my parachute harness over my vest and placed my helmet in a cloth helmet bag, along with a card that listed my mission number, takeoff time, radio call signals, and Alpha frequency for both receiving and sending radio transmissions. I would carry all that onto the plane. I also made sure I had my flashlight and earplugs and checked my life-support gear.

Just before we had entered the locker room, Wilbur had asked me to verify our search-and-rescue (SAR) plan, in case, he said, one of us had to eject. Because the likelihood of an air accident seemed so small, not all pilots bothered to review their SAR plan in detail before every sortie. It was something you ran through in three minutes. Wilbur, however, was a perfectionist. He insisted that each of us recite the full procedure in detail, starting with the moment we had to parachute to the ground and hide from the enemy. We also reviewed the two radio frequencies for communicating. One was called Guard, the international distress channel, on which the whole world could hear you, including the enemy. The other was Alpha, one of the two SAR channels on our handheld radios, the frequency of which we changed often to give us more privacy than we had on the Guard channel. Wilbur and I agreed on a secret code if we had to radio in our GPS coordinates over Alpha, so that the good guys could find us but not the enemy. Taking the extra time to run through every detail satisfied Wilbur and left the plan fresh in our minds.

Though I had no idea of it at the time, something else happened that morning that may have helped prepare me for the ordeal ahead. An article entitled "The Will to Survive" was posted in the men's room, which was near the ops desk. For some reason, I had never read it. This morning, however, I had a few extra minutes, and I found my eyes skimming the article. It told the stories of two similar survival crises with very different outcomes. One story was about a man traveling in the Arizona desert who, injured in an accident, got lost and went for eight days without water. By the time rescuers found him, he was so dehydrated that everyone concluded he should have been dead. But his will to survive was so incredibly strong, he probably could have gone even longer without water.

The other story was about a civilian pilot in Alaska whose single-engine plane went down on a frozen lake bed. The man radioed for help but wasn't sure whether anyone heard his transmission. He wasn't far from shore, and from his footprints it appeared to rescuers that he had walked toward the shore but had never bothered to build a shelter or start a fire. Instead, he returned to the plane, picked up the gun that was in his survival kit, and killed himself. Rescue helicopters came twenty-four hours later, having heard his radio transmission. Because he had assumed the worst, because he had given up on himself, the man had thrown away his chance to survive.

For the briefest of seconds I wondered how strong my will was. But the question dissolved into more immediate concerns. The planes were ready, and it was time for our sorties.

One of the last things Wilbur and I did was chow down on a pizza, which we shared with some enlisted men. Having skipped breakfast, I was hungry and could have eaten a lot more.

Moving toward the van that would take us to our F-16s, I discovered I'd left my flight jacket back in my locker. I'd never been that forgetful before a mission, but rushing back and wrestling off my vest and other gear so that I could put on my jacket seemed unnecessary. Climate control in the F-16 was perfect. You could turn the heat up or down with a dial. I decided I could live without my jacket for one flight.

The van driver dropped off Wilbur and me by our planes. We made separate visual inspections of our aircraft before climbing into the cockpit. The 47-foot-long, 30,000-pound (fully loaded with fuel), single-seat, single-jet-engine F-16 was a marvel of engineering. It had been designed and built by General Dynamics back in 1978 and had gone through several updates over the years. The F-16 was small and compact compared with other fighter jets, but it was very popular with air forces around the world. More than half of our own air force's fighter planes were F-16s. Its weapons and defense systems made it superior to the Soviet MiG, one of its famous competitors for speed and power, and its long-term safety record spoke for its keen performance.

In my years of training before the Air Force, I had piloted almost a dozen types of civilian aircraft. I was rated to fly all of them, but none was more exciting or challenging than the F-16. Besides its smooth ride, it was smarter than Einstein. The F-16's brain center was an advanced computer inside the aircraft. A separate targeting pod could be added to the underbelly of the plane that would "talk" to the computer inside. This pod relayed information through my cockpit instruments that helped me find and lock on hostile targets that were miles

11

away. The targeting pod also could send out a laser beam to mark ground targets, which would help me guide my bombs more accurately. In addition, the F-16 carried an electronic countermeasures pod, which could block or jam enemy radar.

Under its smooth, gunmetal gray skin, the F-16 was designed to hold as many weapons, and as much fuel, as possible without hurting the plane's speed and ability to maneuver in the air. Under each wing was an air-to-air missile along with a 500-pound laser-guided bomb; each wingtip held another air-to-air missile. In the fuselage was a 20-mm Gatling gun, for use if an enemy plane came within close range or if I had to fly low to fire at a land target. Since our missions over Bosnia were more defensive than offensive, and because we wanted to be as light and as fuel efficient as possible, we didn't carry the four additional 500-pound bombs an F-16 normally held. They were hardly necessary. While I wasn't looking forward to combat, I knew I was ready for any hostile situation.

One unique feature of the F-16 was the one-piece bubble canopy that sat over the entire cockpit. Its sleek shape acted as a perfect windscreen, and it allowed a pilot clear views in almost all directions. For strength and resilience the canopy was made of a high-tech material called polycarbonate. If an unfortunate bird was to find itself on collision course with the canopy—a common problem in the sky—the polycarbonate wouldn't shatter dangerously the way the old cast-acrylic canopies had. Instead, it would absorb the impact of the bird by bending inward, then magically reshape itself. It may sound silly, but to make sure the polycarbonate canopies were "bird safe," the aircraft manufacturer tested them by shooting four-pound frozen chickens out of a high-speed cannon, hitting the canopies at over 300 miles per hour! While safe from a shattering canopy, a pilot in the air still faced the danger of the momentary dent left by the flying bird. If a plane was moving at 500 miles or more, a good-sized turkey vulture could actually hit the canopy hard enough to knock out a pilot. That's why it was necessary to maintain some distance—the size of your fist, at least—between your head and the bottom of the canopy.

The cockpit of the F-16 was not exactly designed with extra luxury room. As I climbed in and straddled my legs around the center instrument console, I placed my feet on the rudder pedals and strapped myself in. The snug cockpit fits like a glove. It also makes you feel as if you're part of the sky. Unlike the cockpits in other fighters, the F-16's cockpit projects out and over the front of the plane, so most of the fuselage is below and behind you. With the gorgeous views from the one-piece canopy, sometimes you're tempted to forget you're even in a plane.

I plugged my air hose into my G suit. When I started

making sharp turns in the sky and the G forces kicked in, the air hose would automatically turn on and fill the various pockets or bladders of my G suit—two on each leg and one at my stomach. Filled with air, the G suit was another way to help keep blood from flowing from my head into the rest of my body. After inserting the air hose, I hooked my shoulder harness clips to my parachute risers. Clipped to my hips was a canvas package that contained a survival rucksack, a deflated life raft, and a small "hit and run" secondary survival kit. This package was part of the seat pan on which I sat. If I ever had to eject from the plane and use my parachute, the seat pan, along with my entire seat, would fall away, but the canvas package would stay clipped to my hips. It contained the gear that, if the parachute landed me safely, I would need to survive.

After fastening my lap belt, I put on my helmet and oxygen mask. With a thumbs-up signal to the ground crew chief to pull away my cockpit ladder, I made a final review of my lineup card, which detailed my flight mission information.

"Fore and aft clear . . . fire guard posted . . . chocks in place?" I asked over the intercom to the crew chief. Chocks were blocks that were placed in front of the wheels so that the plane wouldn't roll.

"Roger," he answered. "All ready for run-up."

I turned on two switches, one for electrical power and

the other to start a small engine that would, in a few moments, turn over the main jet engine. My left hand moved the throttle from Off to Idle. With a whine building to a roar, the main engine, a GE-100, came to life. After more ground checks, one by one I activated all of the plane's systems.

Once I was in the air, the instruments on my center console would indicate airspeed, altitude, attitude (the plane's reference to the horizon), and bearing. Just over my left knee, a radar screen would show me if there were any no-fly-zone intruders. Above that screen sat my threat warning system, which would let me know if my plane had been tagged by hostile radar. If that happened, I knew there was a real possibility of a missile attack. A rectangular keyboard pad was perched above the instrument console, along with buttons for my two radios. There was also a head-up display (HUD), a clear glass panel directly in front of me, that gave additional information to help with navigation and weapons targeting.

After exchanging more hand signals with the ground crew chief, I was directed to move my plane forward. I fell in line behind Wilbur. There was a last-minute stop to allow for a final systems and weapons check by the ground crew. Finally, we were cleared for takeoff and I taxied onto the runway.

No matter how many flights I'd made—and I'd flown more than 800 hours in an F-16—each takeoff was an act of magic that never grew old. Maybe it goes back to my fascination with speed, or just a deep appreciation of the F-16. As I moved my plane to one side of Wilbur's so that his jet exhaust wouldn't blow on me, Wilbur received takeoff clearance for both of us from air traffic control. Then Wilbur gave me a signal to turn up my engine to ninety percent of full power. After I scanned my instruments for any last-second warning lights, I watched Wilbur roll down the runway at full thrust. Within seconds, an orange flame shot out the back of his plane, indicating that his afterburner had kicked in. The power of a takeoff is so incredible that, even if you're a good distance behind and to one side of the departing jet, your plane shakes like a leaf. By the time I had blinked and straightened in my seat, Wilbur had become a small red dot against a deep cobalt blue sky.

I waited twenty seconds after Wilbur started his takeoff roll—this was a necessary time span so that we wouldn't collide in the clouds—before I took my feet off the brakes and pushed my throttle forward. Gliding smoothly down the runway with a sure, steady motion, I pushed further on the throttle until I was at full afterburner. This injected fuel into the engine's hot exhaust stream and created thrust, the power for a quick takeoff. I felt as if I were being shot into space with a slingshot.

Liftoff speed was 200 miles an hour, which I had reached in a matter of seconds. I made a lightning-speed check of my instruments to be certain there were no systems failures or need for an emergency landing. In the next second, before the plane reached 330 miles an hour, I pulled up my landing gear. That speed is critical. The landing gear is fragile, and if a pilot waits too long to pull it up, high air speeds can do serious damage when the gear is in motion. Everything in the F-16 happens in what seems like microseconds. Reflexes mean a lot.

I looked at my watch, an old but expensive Rolex that had been a gift from my dad several years before. It was 1:15 P.M., Aviano time, and I was feeling on top of the world.

TWO

I broke through scattered cloud cover at 12,000 feet and stared into a magnificently clear sky. I had already locked on to Wilbur with my radar, and now fixed my airspeed so that I would stay two miles behind him. At our current speed, we could cover two miles in all of twenty seconds.

"Two is visual," I radioed to Wilbur on our interflight frequency. This meant that I had him in my sights.

"Clear to rejoin," he replied. We were now over the Adriatic Sea and would be in Bosnian airspace in about fifteen minutes. I closed the gap between us until we were in fingertip formation. We flew side by side, separated only by a few feet, and held our positions. This allowed Wilbur and me to make a visual inspection of each other's aircraft, to make sure that there were no fluid leaks and that all external systems were working. We also tested our chaff and flares, both part of the F-16's defense system. Chaff was a substance like tinfoil that was discharged from the plane to give enemy radar a false image to read. Flares were discharged to try to attract incoming heat-seeking missiles away from our planes.

Everything looked perfect. Inspection over, we moved

into a formation known as tactical line abreast. As the wingman, I flew a mile and a half from Wilbur and about 2,000 feet above him. Wilbur's role was to lead our mission and to be the eyes and ears of our two-ship element. My responsibility was to maintain the basic flight formation and to support Wilbur in his decisions during the mission. We were now at 27,000 feet and cruising at 500 miles an hour, an altitude and speed similar to those of a commercial jetliner. The only difference was, we were flying over unfriendly territory.

Our flight pattern carried us over the lush, green boundary separating Croatia and Bosnia, just south of a city named Bihać. We were running into a fair amount of clouds, and the air was choppy, but we decided to establish our combat air patrol, or "cap." We patrolled the skies by flying an oval pattern, similar to the shape of a race-track, with each leg covering about twenty-five miles. Each oval took about eight minutes to complete, including making the two 180-degree counterclockwise turns. Flying the same pattern over and over might sound boring, but you never knew who would try to enter the no-fly zone. This was called our "vul" time, when we were vulnerable over hostile territory. A few minutes after we started our vul time, our radars showed a low-flying aircraft to the west, near the Udbina airfield. This was the stronghold of the Krajanian Serbs, and they were an aggressive bunch. Sixteen months earlier, despite NATO planes protecting the no-fly zone, the Krajanian Serbs had boldly launched an air attack against Muslim sites in Bosnia. To show that we meant business, NATO pilots had had to shoot down four Serbian jets.

The lone plane stayed clear of the no-fly zone, avoiding any hostile action by me.

After about an hour of combat air patrol, we began to run low on fuel. The F-16 uses an enormous amount of fuel—a mixture of kerosene and gasoline, about 10,000 pounds for every hour and a half of flying. That's the same as a car getting two or three miles to the gallon. Following Wilbur's lead, I headed back over the Adriatic to meet our specially equipped Boeing 707 plane. This was our airborne gas station. While I "parked" on the tanker's wing, Wilbur took a position directly under the fuselage of the 707. As we all flew at the same speed, Wilbur flipped a toggle switch to open his fuel door, which sat right behind his cockpit. At the same time, the operator of the 707 extended a boom and probe—like a gas hose—into Wilbur's open fuel tank. Then it was just like any other gas station. The pump was turned on, and you waited until your gauge showed Full.

After Wilbur's turn it was mine, and I passed the seven-minute refueling time talking to the tanker crew on my intercom. I discovered one of the crew was a former "Juvat," a pilot with the Eightieth Fighter Squadron in Korea, with whom I had served a tour of duty. We Juvats, past and present, were a tight bunch. We even had a squadron coin that summed up our close bonds. The coin read: "You will always be a Juvat no matter where you go."

"Audentes fortuna juvat," I called out to my fellow Juvat as I left the tanker. The Latin words were our squadron's motto: "Fortune favors the bold."

For our second vul time, Wilbur led me slightly north of our last location, in search of better weather. Finding a relatively clear patch of sky, we settled into our routine. Instead of running our ovals northwest and southeast as we had last time, we rotated to due west and east. I was 1,000 feet above Wilbur and continually moved my eyes between the sky and the dials and digital instruments in front of me. While we had no reason to worry about anything specific, we knew to stay far away from the Bosnian Serbs' SAM rings to the north and to the east. SAMs—surface-to-air missiles—were a definite threat to an F-16, even with our high-tech defense systems.

What Wilbur and I had no way of knowing was that a Bosnian Serb unit had secretly trucked a SAM battery into an area underneath where we were patrolling. And their missiles were already lined up, ready to fire at us.

The first sign of trouble came when Wilbur's threat warning system showed a blip on his screen. He had been "spiked," spotted by radar on the ground. By itself, this was no major concern. In Bosnia, radar was extremely common as a general tracking device, much like traffic control centers at major airports. A blip on a screen wasn't necessarily connected with missiles. But the F-16's electronics could pick out different types of radar. Wilbur had been spiked by "acquisition," or threat, radar—the kind that SAM operators liked to use. With threat radar, the enemy can learn enough about a plane's location, speed, and flight pattern to launch a missile in seconds.

"Basher Five-One, mud six, bearing zero-nine-zero," Wilbur radioed to me on our open frequency. He wanted me to know there was possibly threat radar to the east.

"Basher Five-Two naked," I shot back. That told him my threat warning system hadn't picked up anything.

On the same open radio frequency, I listened for Magic, NATO's nearby airborne command center. Equipped with special intel electronics, the airborne center served to help pilots as an early warning system. In touch with spy satellites and U-2 spy planes, Magic could tell Wilbur and me if there was active radar from the SAM rings to the north and to the east as well as in any other location. If the radar was coming from the north and the east, we didn't have to worry because we were out of their missiles' range. The blip on Wilbur's threat warning system would have been a false alarm.

It took Magic only seconds to get back to us. "Basher Five One," a calm voice called over our radios, "your mud six report is uncorrelated."

Magic was saying that they couldn't really confirm where the radar was coming from. Cautiously, Wilbur and I continued to fly our ovals. At exactly 3:03 P.M., Aviano time, *my* threat warning system showed a bright blip. I stared at my console in disbelief. At the same time, an alarm shrilled over my headset. I had been spiked by threat radar.

Forget any threat from the north. This was coming from due east, just like the one Wilbur had picked up. Could it really be a second false alarm? My stomach did a flip.

"Basher Five-Two, mud six, bearing zero-nine-zero," I said into my radio.

"Basher Five-One naked," Wilbur reported back.

Our roles had been reversed. It was now my turn to be hunted. I knew I had to prepare myself for the worst. Through my canopy I scanned the skies for any evidence of a missile. The actual rocket that fires a SAM leaves a trail of white smoke. That smoke is a pilot's only chance to make a visual identification. Once the rocket turns off, the smoke stops. Then the missile sails on toward its target, silent and deadly, at a speed almost twice as fast as my F-16.

Seeing nothing in the sky, my eyes swam back to the video display on my threat warning system. The bright blip had not gone away, which meant I was still being spiked. A moment later, a second alarm blared over my headset. My glance jumped back to my screen. A new warning was there, brighter than the one before.

This was all happening in seconds. Split seconds. But it was long enough for me to understand I had just been locked up by a target-tracking radar. This was the type that guided a missile to its target. While I didn't know it, Magic had received information from a spy satellite that there were missiles right below Wilbur and me, but because of a garbled radio communication, we never got the message. It hardly mattered. My instrument panel had already delivered the bad news.

I was in somebody's deadly sights. As I thought out the meaning of those words, I realized a missile might already have been launched. I was angry that we had all been outsmarted by the enemy, but I tried to stay calm. This was what our years of training had prepared us for, and I was ready.

A programmed voice from the plane's computer system rang out over my headset. "Counter, counter."

A second later, a brilliant red flash lit up the sky between Wilbur and me. A missile had passed between us, just missing us both. My heart sped up. I knew that SAMs were usually launched in packages of two. The chances were likely that another missile was already in the air, coming straight at me. As the adrenaline pumped through my veins, my thumb traveled down to the button that would release my chaff and flares. At the same time, I thought about pushing my aircraft into a series of steep climbs and dives to avoid the missile.

I had time to do neither. What happened in the next tick of a second, I'm not sure. Wilbur would later tell me that he had screamed over the radio, "Missiles in the air!" I never heard him. What I did hear was a thunderous roar that almost shattered my eardrums. Then came a blow like nothing I had ever felt. It was like getting rear-ended by an 18-wheeler with a rocket tied to its front grill.

The missile had found its mark.

A burst of flames and intense heat spread through my cockpit. I began to pitch and roll wildly. It felt as if a giant hand had reached down, grabbed me with brute force, and shaken me in a frenzy. What was left of my plane was like a straw in the wind, totally out of control.

For all its space-age electronics, its supersonic speed, its defensive powers, the F-16 is not perfect. In the blink of an eye, it can be turned from the prince of the skies into a burning scrap heap of wire and twisted metal. The missile had blindsided me, coming up through cloud cover below. It had struck the plane's underbelly, hitting one of the fuel tanks and cutting my F-16 in two. It took me another moment to understand. The nose and cockpit had broken away—and I was now in a free fall to Earth.

As I spun out of control, I worried about blacking out from the sudden and unexpected G forces. I watched my console break and twist apart before me. My mind was outracing my ability to react. Flames from the exploding gas tank had found a crack between my oxygen mask and visor. They had also reached the back of my neck. Part of me was waiting for the cockpit to explode. Somehow, the heat and the pain and the insanity of the moment focused my thoughts.

Dear God, I prayed, *please don't let me die now—don't let me die from this.*

I gazed down, through the flames, and saw a fat yellow handle attached to my seat. The handle pushed up between my legs, bigger than life, staring at me like the miracle I took it to be. The beautiful words stamped across the top were impossible to miss, even in the fire and smoke: PULL TO EJECT.

I had no idea how much time had passed since the missile had struck. In reality it had been only seconds. It felt like an eternity. I knew I wasn't waiting much longer. For another microsecond, I worried that my damaged canopy wouldn't open, or if it did, that the seat wouldn't eject. But I really didn't have time to worry.

My left hand dropped down to the handle, and I pulled with all my might.

THREE

Strictly speaking, birds and insects are the only creatures born to fly. But I was ready to join them in the sky at a very early age.

Before we moved to Spokane, my family lived in Long Beach, California, where my dad had a private pilot's license. At age six, I flew with him in a snappy red-and-white two-seater Cessna 150 to Catalina Island, twenty-six miles away. The 150 was a slow, steady machine, nothing glamorous, but for my first voyage it felt as if I were moving faster than a speeding bullet. Below, the tiny dots of houses and swimming pools slipped by in seconds. As we headed out over the Pacific and I saw the gray waves crashing in formation against the shore, I thought there was no other place to be but up in the heavens. After we landed, the Catalina airport tower honored me with a certificate for my first flight, a piece of paper I proudly signed and have kept to this day.

Even before my first flight, just the sight of a plane in the sky inspired dreams of travel and adventure. Growing up in the late sixties and seventies, I moved from Brooklyn, New York, where I was born, to Long Beach, then to Ridgewood, New Jersey, and finally, at age nine, to Spokane, Washington. My sister, Stacy, was born exactly three years after me, and my brother, Paul, about one year after Stacy. I greeted my sister's arrival in the world—and her very nerve for being born on the same date as I—by throwing balls at her head while she slept in her crib. Maybe I just wanted her to be a boy. When Paul came along, three turned out to be a good number.

As leader of the pack, I was forever convincing Stacy and Paul to join me in different fantasy games. Flying together to some distant island or conquering rugged, ice-faced mountains was pretty typical. We spent as much time as we could outdoors. If my parents took us to the ocean or the mountains, that was special; if not, a city park suited us just fine. I liked things physical, whether it was riding my bike or chasing baby-sitters around the house.

Even in my quiet moments, sitting down with a book, I was focused on the outdoors. My favorite stories had to do with exotic wildlife, particularly large cats and reptiles, and their incredible habitats. At age nine I joined the Cub Scouts and, later, the Webelos. In the Scouts, learning about animals, nature, and wilderness survival earned me badges and arrows for my uniform. I looked forward the most to Scout weekends with my dad. Although it never happened to us, being lost in the mountains, building one's own shelter from scratch, starting a fire from a pair of twigs, and using a compass to find one's way out seemed as though it would be the greatest adventure possible.

With Stacy and Paul, I spent a fair amount of time in front of the television, but not just to pass the hours. Any action movie or adventure series with a war setting was "required" viewing. Because my father had served with the U.S. Marines as a medical doctor, the military was of great interest to me. When my parents had their friends over for a party, if someone had a military story to tell—especially a military *flying* story—I was hard to shoo away. At some point I grew fascinated with the basic mechanics of flight—how an engine or rudder worked—and how fast a jet plane could really go. I did a lot of my learning by observing and talking with adults. I was always amazed by how much some people knew about things that were a complete mystery to me, and I wanted to learn everything I could.

At age twelve, I attended junior high school in Spokane. My fantasy life continued with heavy doses of Dungeons & Dragons, but my interest in sports also blossomed. I played in neighborhood after-school football games and took karate lessons. Martial arts captured my attention to the point that I pleaded with my parents to let me move by myself to Atlanta so that I could study under a special ninja instructor. My request was turned down, but my enthusiasm for looking and acting like a ninja didn't fade. The highlight of my summers was a

YMCA sleep-away camp in the mountains of northeastern Washington. At Camp Reed, I was definitely in my element. Whether taking rugged hikes or learning night navigation by the stars, I had such a great time I was sorry when it was time to leave.

Back at home, if not palling around with my brother and sister or kids in the neighborhood, I spent time with my dad. Knowing my interest in sports and things mechanical, he gave me advice one fall when I built my own race car to enter in the local Soap Box Derby. I didn't win, but I was fascinated with the idea of how fast I could make a car go. Speed, in fact, was getting into my blood. When my dad later took the family on vacation, we went to the famous Cyclone roller coaster on Coney Island in Brooklyn. I jumped into the front row and threw my hands fearlessly into the air with every terrifying plunge. I don't know how many rides I took before I was dragged off under protest. Later I became a black-diamond alpine skier, fearless no matter how icy or steep the slope in front of me.

With the fascination by speed came a deeper interest in sports, and with sports came competition. Whether it was soccer or football or skiing, I was never the type to be envious or jealous of those who had more talent. But I did like to compete against myself, setting goals and then pushing myself to do better. One winter, on a family vacation at Snowmass, Colorado, I learned that you could earn a gold medal by trying a particularly challenging run and then entering your time against other skiers. My first attempt was okay, but nowhere near as fast as others my age. There was no limit on how many times you could make the run, so I did it over and over—maybe ten times altogether—until I was satisfied with my time. I came back with the silver medal, not the gold, but what was important was that I had tried my best. Later, when I became interested in high-powered rifles and entered several competitions for marksmanship, any trophies I took home were nice, but the endless hours of practice and sharpening my skills gave me the most pleasure.

When I was around fourteen, on my first flight with my dad since our trip to Catalina, we flew a straight-tail Beechcraft Bonanza to Kalispell, Montana, for duck hunting. In the middle of the flight, as we passed over towering crags and peaks, Dad turned to me in the co-pilot's seat. In the most casual of voices he suggested I take the controls for a few minutes. After overcoming my shock, I forgot the scenery and wrapped my hands around the steering yoke. That was when I realized I had been wanting to take control all along.

The trust my dad showed in me by putting me in control of the plane was as important as the thrill of piloting it. As wild and headstrong as I could sometimes be, my parents, particularly my dad, rarely lost their patience. And they never lost their faith in me. As long as my activity was reasonably safe, they let me do whatever I wanted. And no one lectured me when I made mistakes, as long as I learned from them and took pride in what I did.

Pride, in fact, was the glue that held the O'Grady family together. My father's mother had come over from Ireland without a penny and worked menial jobs to get by. She married a New York City policeman, and together they raised a family through difficult times. On my mother's side, my grandfather was the oldest of five children. After his father died, he supported the whole family with odd jobs—I don't think he was even a teenager yet. Later he put himself through college and medical school and became one of Brooklyn's first children's heart specialists. As if that weren't enough work, he and my grandmother also raised nine children, including two doctors, two teachers, an engineer, and three business professionals. Hard work, patriotism, a belief in oneself, and support for each other—those are the core O'Grady values.

Besides being patriotic, my dad was something of a historian. When our family moved from one coast to another, or just took a cross-country car trip, Dad never missed the opportunity to teach Stacy, Paul, and me. We saw Gettysburg, Manassas, Plymouth, Jamestown, Mount Rushmore . . . and Dad was our tour guide. It was no wonder I fell under the spell of some of the giants of American history. Andrew Jackson and Abraham Lincoln were at the top of my list for their ability to lead and for their taking of risks to decide the fate of the country. I liked their stubbornness, too. That is another O'Grady trait. If you pursue something, pursue it with all your heart.

After I entered high school, I began to think seriously of the military as a profession. A lot of kids my age didn't care about patriotism or serving their country, but my friends and I had a different view. We never understood why Vietnam veterans were treated so poorly by the American public or why the military had such a black eye from the Vietnam conflict. Maybe I was old-fashioned, or was modeling myself after my dad, but to me no goal was more honorable than joining the military. With my love of flying, the U.S. Air Force became my new focus.

I was feeling very grown-up. I tried to convince my parents to let me convert our basement family room into my personal apartment. I could have my own space, I explained, and come and go freely, staying out of their hair. The idea was politely rejected, along with my suggestion—when I had my first driver's license—that my parents buy me a Ferrari sports car. No matter. Entering high school, I let them know I was mature enough to handle any problems that came my way. They were kind enough to nod and say nothing.

While I had many good friends, I was hardly part of

the in crowd at Lewis and Clark High School in Spokane. Serious about my future in the military, for a while
I considered transferring to a high-school military academy. In the end, I stayed at Lewis and Clark and worked
toward my goals. In academics, I took home decent
grades, but I was far from a whiz. In athletics, I had some
skills, particularly in soccer, but I was no natural. Nothing came easily for me. I had to put in twice the effort
that most kids did to achieve the same results.

I was no star, but because I was such a big dreamer, I
decided that besides soccer, I would add football to my
after-school schedule. I thought the really cool guys
played football. Because of my relatively small size, there
weren't too many positions I could seriously consider. But
with my soccer skills and after much practice, I made the
varsity football team as a placekicker.

All season I was stranded on the bench—the coach let
the starters do the kicking—until the biggest game of the
year, against archrival Gonzaga Prep. It was an important
game, not just for the prestige of having bragging rights
for the year, but because I had briefly attended Gonzaga
as a freshman and wanted to show off to my former
classmates. Maybe the coach knew, because just after we
had scored a touchdown, he ordered me into the game. I
looked at him from the other end of the bench as if there
might be a mistake.

"O'Grady," he repeated, "get in there and kick the extra point." I was so nervous as I trotted onto the field that when the ball was finally snapped to the holder, I was late in my timing. My kick got blocked. This had been my chance to be a hero, and I had flubbed it. I was so embarrassed and frustrated that I did a spontaneous frontward flip right on the field, which gave my coaches a good laugh when they reviewed the game film the next day. I never got to kick again.

My pride took longer to heal than my body, but I learned an important lesson. I didn't have to win popularity contests to be happy. If I did what I wanted—and not what I thought the crowd wanted—and if I did it well, I would have respect for myself.

That summer, with Dad's encouragement, I put in the hours to earn my private pilot's license, flying out of nearby Felts Field. I can't boast that I was an immediate success. Like everything else I had tried, flying, particularly my first solo, didn't always go smoothly. Rushing down the runway in my small plane, I looked over to my instructor; his seat was empty. Only then did I remember that this was a solo. I was a bundle of nerves the entire flight, and my landing included three hair-raising bounces, as if I were a rubber ball. But I passed my test, and when I received my license, I felt great.

I applied for admission to the United States Air Force

Academy in Colorado Springs, Colorado, that fall. I was proud of my planning. The academy would further my dream of serving my country. Once I had my officer's commission, it would be on to different air force flight schools for advanced training. My future was set—or so I thought. I had my congressman's nomination to the academy and decent enough grades. My verbal SAT score, however, fell just short of the admissions requirement. There were no second chances. The United States Air Force Academy turned me down.

I gave myself a pep talk, pretending the rejection didn't matter, and in front of my parents I acted as if this setback were minor. My real goal was not the United States Air Force Academy, it was the United States Air Force, and I could always take ROTC courses at a regular college to earn my commission as an officer. But the truth was, my self-confidence had taken a beating. I was deeply disappointed because I had placed my hopes in being accepted to the United States Air Force Academy. Now that I had been rejected, I enrolled at my second-choice school, the University of Washington in Seattle.

There I jumped from one area of study to another, changing my mind four times. I also joined a college men's club called a fraternity, where I goofed off too much and didn't get my schoolwork done. My ROTC courses were the only thing that meant anything. During the second trimester of my sophomore year, without telling my family, I dropped out of school, made my way to Sun Valley, Idaho, and became a ski bum. This was one of the most unfocused periods of my life. I did finally get back to Seattle, and did reenroll at the University of Washington, but I still didn't know what I was doing with my life. When I got together with my dad, I didn't have to pretend otherwise with him. He just knew.

"What do you want to do?" he asked calmly.

"I want to fly," I said.

We had several discussions about my future, how to get my feet back on the ground—or in the air. Dad had always believed that there was more than one path to the same destination. A friend of his recommended that I apply to Embry-Riddle Aeronautical University in Daytona Beach, Florida. It wasn't the United States Air Force Academy, but I could take ROTC courses and earn a degree in aeronautics, the science of flight and aircraft operation. I could also grab a lot of flying time and earn ratings in different aircraft. Embry-Riddle accepted me as a sophomore for the fall of 1986. When I was informed that its Florida campus was fully enrolled, I was disappointed but didn't let the news stop me. There was still another path to take. Embry-Riddle has a smaller satellite campus in Prescott, Arizona.

Prescott was a far cry from the snow-capped mountains

and green valleys of the Northwest or the partying atmosphere of Daytona Beach. It took some time to get used to the Southwestern desert and my new academic schedule. But I studied hard, did well in my major, aeronautical science, and put extra time into ROTC. The summer after my sophomore year, I had my first military experience, at Lowry Air Force Base in Denver, taking four weeks of field training that included a two day survival course. Although it was only forty-eight hours, the survival course was intense. When our instructor showed us the joys of eating ants, I decided I'd rather go hungry.

Back at Embry-Riddle I earned nine different flight ratings, from seaplane to commercial multiengine to glider to certified flight instructor. I also won a rare pilot scholarship from the U.S. Air Force, which pleased my parents. The scholarship meant my last two years of college would be completely paid for by the federal government.

A few months later, I signed a long-term contract with the U.S. Air Force, agreeing to a nine-year commitment in exchange for the best pilot training in the world. I was happy with the deal. I was happy with Embry-Riddle and the education I was receiving. Mostly, I was happy with myself. Maybe I'd never have the glamour of a degree from the United States Air Force Academy, but in Prescott I'd learned to be independent and self-reliant.

By the summer of 1989, I had graduated with special

honors and earned my commission as a second lieutenant in the U.S. Air Force. Best of all, I had been accepted to the Euro-NATO Joint Jet Training Program at Sheppard Air Force Base in Texas.

My flight plan was back in the right direction.

FOUR

With one tug of that fat yellow handle, I knew one of two things was going to happen: either I was going to be tossed free of the plane, or the equipment somehow wasn't going to work and my life was going to be over.

I had never ejected from a plane before. I had studied the procedure in school, but obviously our training didn't include ditching a $20 million F-16 for the sake of practice. All I knew was that it wasn't the safest sport in the world. In training we heard stories of pilots who had ejected and ended up in wheelchairs; some had been killed outright. When you rocket out of a plane, screaming through the sky at 500 miles an hour, or are tossed into 100-mile-per-hour gale-force winds, anything can happen. The G forces you pull, which can run up to twenty, might damage your spinal column; you could lose a leg or an arm if not sitting properly in your chair when you eject; or the canopy might not open above you.

But no matter what the risks, if your plane was like mine, on fire and plummeting to earth in a hurry, you pulled the handle.

So I did.

In a microsecond the bubble canopy above me exploded off the cockpit and fell free of the plane. In another microsecond the small rocket under my seat shot me straight up out of the cockpit and into the cold, thin air of space.

Spinning through the air, I watched what was left of my F-16 fall away in an exploding fireball. I had escaped a certain, terrible death. I had used up another of my nine lives. My plane, slowed by the SAM hit, had been going less than 500 miles an hour. The ejection seat and its rocket had done their job. I hadn't had time to think about tucking in my arms and legs for a textbook ejection. I'd just reacted. To wait even another fraction of a second could have meant serious injury or death.

As I tumbled out of control through space, I knew I was still in great danger. I was five miles above Earth and falling like a stone, waiting for my parachute to open automatically. Worse, I was upside down, my body parallel to the ground, belly facing down. I couldn't move very well because I was still strapped into my ejection seat, which included a back and headrest. A patchwork quilt of farmland lay below me.

I took stock of my situation. My cheeks stung from the cold air and, I guessed, the fire in the cockpit. Hitting the strong winds outside the plane, I lost my visor, the flashlight clipped to my vest, and even my camouflaged name patch, which left only the Velcro pad behind it. The heel of my left boot had been ripped during the ejection. I felt okay, but I couldn't be sure of the extent of my injuries, if any, until I landed.

What concerned me most was my parachute. It wouldn't open until I dropped to an altitude of 14,000 feet. There, the oxygen level and temperature would be more agreeable. That's when the sensors in my "smart" seat would activate the parachute and my seat would fall away, letting me float cleanly to Earth. This sounded fine, but I was still worried. What if the parachute, made of paper-thin nylon, had been damaged by the missile blast or the cockpit fire . . . what if it just didn't work?

I was falling at a rate of about one mile every two minutes, or about 2,500 feet every sixty seconds. That may sound fast, but I had a long way to go before I reached 14,000 feet. My nerves were as thin as the oxygen level. Suddenly, I didn't want to wait to see if my parachute was going to work. My response was partly that of a pilot who wasn't used to hanging around, who liked to make things happen. But I also thought that if the parachute wasn't going to open and I was headed for a grisly death, it was better to know sooner than later. I wasn't sure what I would do, but I'd have more time to figure something out.

I said another prayer. With a tug on my seat handle— one that could open my chute *now*—I heard a wonderful *pop*, and instantly my speed began to slow. I did my best to look up, over my headrest. A drogue chute—a small chute whose job it was to stabilize me—had been released first. Seconds later, with another, louder pop, the main parachute was gloriously billowing above me. I was still strapped into my chair and headrest, but at least I was right side up. The ground was where it should have been, below me, and the sky was above. I moved my arms and legs. Nothing seemed broken. I thanked God again.

Despite the fear of not being able to breathe at the high altitude, I pulled off my helmet and oxygen mask and let them drop to Earth. My face was really burning, and I craved the relief of cool air. The cold blasts felt wonderful, and I wasn't getting dizzy in the thin altitude. In fact, my mind was alert enough to realize I had made one slight miscalculation. While I thought I'd been in a free fall for minutes, in fact the time span since ejecting from the plane had been much shorter. I'd only dropped about 3,000 feet before I opened my parachute. I was still 24,000 feet in the air, and now traveling at a rate of less than 1,000 feet a minute. That meant it would be almost half an hour before I hit the ground!

That was plenty of time for the Serbs to spot me and give chase. As a strong gust began to blow me sideways, I had no idea where I would land. The farmland below looked wide and open, without many places to hide. I could see the good-sized city of Bosanski Petrovac a few miles to the west and a highway that ran out of the city to

43

the east. Farther south, beyond the road, thick black smoke coiled into the air and a ring of flames lit up the field below—the spot where my ill-fated plane had crashed. Soldiers in the area as well as locals might already be at the site, training their eyes on the sky. With my parachute above me, I would be as hard to miss as the Goodyear blimp.

Part of me couldn't believe this was happening. Minutes before, I had been safely tucked in my jet, master of the sky. Now my plane burned in a Bosnian forest, and I had been stripped of all my powers. I felt like Superman forced to wear a cape of kryptonite. Suddenly I heard the deep roar of a jet directly above. Wilbur, I thought, and I glanced up eagerly. But there was too much cloud cover for either of us to see the other. I reached for the toggle switch on my seat pan. With a flip of my finger, I could activate a radio beacon on my seat pan and send out a distress signal on the Guard channel. Every radio operator in Bosnia would know I was alive, but so would Wilbur. If I hoped to be rescued, NATO had to be positive that I was alive. They also needed to know my physical location within one nautical mile. Those were the two requirements before any rescue mission could be launched.

I didn't hesitate. I activated the beacon for several seconds. The jet noise faded away. I scrambled for my handheld radio in my survival vest pocket, intent on sending a second signal. But the radio was in a plastic bag, in case I had to ditch into the sea. What if I fumbled everything in my eagerness to make contact and the radio fell to the ground? I had a backup radio in my survival kit, but I didn't feel like taking any chances. I left the radio in my vest. There was nothing more I could do. I had no idea if Wilbur, or anyone else, friend or foe, had picked up my signal.

Whether Wilbur knew I was alive or not, I was on my own for now. I was about to land in hostile territory. I knew from intel that I couldn't count on finding any nice guys in Bosnia. At this very moment someone could have a rifle trained on me, waiting for an order to squeeze the trigger. Or soldiers could be hidden in a nearby farmhouse, waiting for the chance to capture me. I remembered the U.S. Military Code of Conduct, which all members of the U.S. armed forces are sworn to uphold: I was never to surrender of my own free will. Instead, I was to evade the enemy at all costs. If I was captured, I would resist and try to escape. Under no circumstances would I help the enemy in any way.

At 14,000 feet, the sensor in my ejection seat did its job, and my seat and headrest fell to Earth. My seat pan also fell away, leaving only the canvas package clipped to my hips. The canvas package then opened automatically, releasing a twenty-five-foot cord with my main rucksack anchored at the bottom. The self-inflating life raft was in the middle, and my hit-and-run auxiliary rucksack was at the top, closest to me. My parachute, of course, had already opened several minutes before. Unlike some of my fellow pilots who had never jumped from a plane, I was pretty comfortable in a parachute. I'd had plenty of practice, five jumps one summer while at Embry-Riddle and five the next summer when I took a three-week airborne training course at Fort Benning, Georgia. When growing up, I'd learned from my father, and from my own limitations, that if you wanted to come anywhere *near* perfection, you had better practice a lot. Whether it was kicking footballs or making a karate move or flying a fighter jet, I did something over and over until I was exhausted.

But strapping on a parachute and leaping from a plane is one of those pursuits where, no matter how many times you practice, no two episodes are the same. Even when you're prepared for it, little things can and usually do go wrong. A line can get entangled around your parachute or you can float right into a tree. I thought of the obvious: when you jump behind enemy lines, that's when you can least afford an error.

As I studied the landscape below, I spotted some hilly, dense woods to the south that I decided would make a good hiding place—so long as I didn't catch my parachute on a tree limb. The woods offered far better cover than open farmland. I reached for the pair of red handles above my head that were attached to the parachute.

These would allow me to change the shape of the para-chute and the way the wind passed through it, which in turn would let me steer in the direction I wanted. But as I grabbed for the handles, I found that one was stuck in the sleeve of the parachute and couldn't be reached. I needed both handles to steer effectively. Helpless, I was going where the wind propelled me.

I gazed down again. A truck with a canvas back—the type used in military convoys—seemed to be following me on the highway below. Without warning it pulled over on the shoulder. A car stopped behind it. I had to assume the worst, that these were hostile forces and, un-less the wind kept carrying me out of their reach, I was in deep trouble.

Dear God, I prayed, *let me land in a safe place, without harm.*

I don't know how many prayers I'd uttered since my plane had been struck. Each prayer seemed more urgent than the previous one, but each one God had answered. It was as if I were using up the rest of my nine lives in record time, and I hadn't even faced the enemy.

Only a thousand feet above the ground, with my eyes still aimed on the truck and car stopped on the highway, I made another mental check of my equipment. Although I had lost my flashlight, I knew my radio was still in my vest, as well as my GPS receiver. My main survival ruck-sack and the hit-and-run secondary kit were attached to the twenty-five-foot cord below me. The life raft dangled below me too, but I'd have no need for that.

As I sailed closer to the ground, I remembered what I had been taught at Fort Benning. In landing, you kept your eyes pointed at the horizon, your legs and feet together, knees slightly bent; once on the ground, you collapsed into a sideways roll. The goal was to cushion your twelve-miles-per-hour landing by using the balls of your feet, your calf, thigh, hip, and upper back.

I said another prayer. The wind whistled through my hair. Then the ground rose up and slammed into me like a rock.

FIVE

I had dropped about half a football field's length from the road. Tumbling on my left side, I rolled to a stop, without getting dragged or entangled by my parachute. Better still, I had landed in an empty clearing of grass that was surrounded by fairly dense woods. Later I would realize how fortunate I was to have released my parachute at 24,000 feet. If I had waited until 14,000 feet, the winds wouldn't have had a chance to carry me this far, and I might have dropped straight into a nearby village.

For the moment I had lost sight of the mysterious convoy truck and car, but I wasn't taking any chances. I had to assume they had watched my landing and were on their way. My mind raced as I released the clips of my parachute harness, then those of the canvas padded kit attached to my hips. All I could think about was getting out of there with the speed of a rabbit.

Set to run, I realized that the plastic bag holding my radio had fallen out of my vest, and the cord attached to it was caught in the parachute lines. Working frantically, I untangled the radio and slipped it back inside my survival vest. My main survival rucksack was at my feet. As the noise of approaching vehicles filled the air, I scooped up the rucksack and began running into the woods, away from the road. In my haste I had left behind my secondary hit-and-run survival kit, which included extra water and other provisions. I also left my parachute, which might have given me protection from the elements, but I wasn't about to drag something so big and obvious through the woods. I knew from my survival training that it was important to be as light on my feet as possible.

Except for the burns on my face, I was amazed by the seemingly good shape I was in, considering the catastrophe I'd survived. As I ran, it didn't seem as though I had any serious injuries. But my legs soon turned stiff and heavy, and I was quickly exhausted. What I failed to grasp was my emotional state. When I had run about a hundred yards from my landing site, I didn't think I could move another step. I dove into the first grove of trees that I thought could provide decent cover. The fear and stress had caught up with me.

Lying on soft, dark earth, I coiled into a semifetal position, drenched in sweat. I could hear vehicles approach my landing site. The first arrivals spoke in low, controlled voices, and I knew more would be coming for the hunt that lay ahead. My morale had never been lower. I was sure I would be captured. How could trained soldiers or even local villagers fail to find a dazed, exhausted American pilot half scared out of his mind, and lying only a couple of hundred feet away? I pulled out my radio and made a last-ditch effort on the Guard channel.

"Hey, Wilbur, this is Zulu," I whispered as clearly as I could, using a nickname that I'd acquired while stationed in Ramstein, Germany, and that Wilbur would know.

I tried Wilbur a second time. There was no reply. As I listened to more vehicles arriving at my landing site, I shut off my radio.

Footsteps began coming my way. My heart sank as I tried to burrow into the dirt, but not before quickly covering my face and ears with my gloves. There was no time to pull out the camouflage paste from my rucksack. The gloves were the same color as my olive drab flight suit, so I hoped I would blend in with the brush.

Within a minute, two men strolled down a path not five feet from my hiding spot. I peeked up warily. One had silver hair; the other looked like his grandson and was no more than eighteen. They were locals, not soldiers, but I knew from intel that many Serb villagers were part of militias and could be just as violent and unpredictable as any uniformed soldier. Hugging the dirt, I was afraid to breathe. Within another minute, two more locals approached my hiding spot—and stopped cold. They were both carrying rifles. About five yards away from me, they traded conversation while their eyes glanced back and forth.

I remembered what one of my survival instructors had taught me. Don't move, no matter what, he had said. Don't assume that the enemy sees you just because you see them. I kept waiting for a stick or a rifle muzzle to jab me in the ribs. Instead, mysteriously, the two men continued down the path, leaving me behind.

I wondered what was next. Within minutes I heard the grinding noise of more trucks around my landing site. Soon the woods were alive with search parties, groups of two or three that fanned out in all directions. Staying glued to the ground, for the next hour I twisted up my head to spy through the low-lying branches. I caught glimpses of men, mostly their legs or backs, as they called to each other and poked and prodded the brush. One pair came within ten feet of me. Like my earlier visitors, these men also wore civilian clothes, but one man had a rifle slung over his arm. Was he out hunting rabbits, or was I the prey of the afternoon?

Seconds later, a shot rang out. I don't know who fired it, but I assumed it was meant for me. Maybe somebody thought they'd spotted me, or they just wanted to flush me out. I closed my eyes, waiting for the next bullet to come my way. I was sure I was facing death. As a young boy, I had attended Catholic schools, had received Communion, and had been confirmed, and I had always felt a close and personal relationship with God. In this dark hour, I began calling on every saint and apostle I knew for protection. I summoned, too, my grandparents and my godmother in heaven for their help. Mostly, I prayed to God, over and over.

I didn't want to die alone, in the middle of nowhere, while everyone I loved and was close to back home had no idea of my fate. That was my worst fear, that no one would know how I had died. I could imagine a U.S. Air Force chaplain appearing at my father's house in Alexandria, Virginia, and delivering the worst news in the world. I could see my father dissolve into tears. My parents were divorced now, but they remained close, and it wasn't hard to imagine the effect that my death would have. The future would cease to exist. My mother, who lived in Seattle with her husband, Joseph, was supposed to meet me in Italy in a week. In July I was going to rendezvous with my brother and sister in Spain. My father was coming for a visit in October. . . .

All that would never happen now.

I prayed. *Our Father who art in Heaven, Hallowed be thy name . . .*

A second shot rang out, followed by the sound of the bullet bouncing off a rock. There were more footsteps, excited voices. I worried about the Ziploc bag that had held my radio and was now stuck under my leg. What if the late afternoon light bounced off it and gave me away?

I was trembling, much too afraid to look up anymore. I was only twenty-nine years old, but I thought I had lived a very full and satisfying life. I had much to be thankful for—a family that was extremely close, countless friends, a career I loved—yet I wasn't ready to cash in my chips. I still had other dreams and goals. I wanted to fall in love with someone, get married, and raise a family. I wouldn't consider my life complete until I'd experienced that happiness. There was so much more I wanted to accomplish.

Thy kingdom come, I kept praying. *Thy will be done, On earth as it is in heaven* . . .

More scattered rifle fire. I hunkered down, afraid that my heart would explode in my chest. It was pounding so hard. I kept waiting. Then I began to cry inside. I didn't think I'd ever make it back to my family and friends.

Back home, on that same afternoon of June 2, representatives of the U.S. Air Force were, in fact, paying visits to both my parents. They talked to my father first, explaining that I had been on a routine but hazardous mission over Bosnia and that my F-16 had been shot down, apparently by a missile. My fellow pilot, Bob "Wilbur" Wright, had not seen a parachute, nor had he made radio or visual contact with me after the incident. Distraught and overwhelmed, my father picked up the phone and called my mother. He had barely given her the news when a separate U.S. Air Force team, consisting of a chaplain and two other officers, approached her front door. My mother saw them through the window as she talked with my father. She put down the phone and let them in.

After a somber greeting from the officer in charge, my mother was handed an official U.S. Air Force letter outlining the same set of facts given to my dad. My mother refused to finish reading the letter. Choking back tears, she bravely told the officers that I was not dead. She had known from the beginning of my career that flying an F-16 was dangerous. She knew the heartbreaking stories of pilots killed on training missions and the families they'd left behind. She knew I was in Italy to fly sorties over hostile territory. Yet she refused to believe that her older son was dead. She told my father, too, and anyone else she spoke with in the next six days. Her faith was constant. It was almost twice as if she wouldn't let me die. Buttressed by her own faith in God, a mother's love for her son is a powerful weapon, more powerful, perhaps, than anything I was up against.

When the air force officers had left my parents' homes, my mom and dad began calling other members of the family. There were a lot of O'Gradys—maybe fifty or sixty of them scattered across the country—and as close as everybody was, in the next six days their bond grew even stronger.

That afternoon, pinned down in my hiding place, I flinched every time a rifle went off or someone thrashed through nearby trees. Minutes crawled by like hours. By nine o'clock, as temperatures began to drop, the area slowly emptied of search parties. I suddenly found myself alone, and I picked up my radio.

"Anyone, Basher Five-Two."

Behind the static there was no response. My strongest urge was to keep trying—like redialing someone's phone number when you get a busy signal—but I worried about the life of the radio batteries. When you just monitored your radio, listening to whoever was on the airwaves, it wasn't that much of a drain on your batteries; but when you transmitted out, speaking into the radio, the batteries took a beating. Altogether, I knew I had about eleven or twelve hours of battery life, and I had no idea how long I would be out there.

I tried to pull my thoughts together—and to make a specific plan for survival—but my mind kept wandering. It was hard not to fantasize about my family or about being back in my apartment for a hot shower and meal or about just sitting around and talking with my pilot buddies. I thought of the transporters on *Star Trek*—maybe Scotty could beam me up. I wondered, too, what I would have been doing right now if I hadn't volunteered for today's flight duty.

There were a lot of what-ifs, but none of them mattered. I had to face reality. And reality told me I couldn't stay here much longer. In the morning, I was sure, soldiers would be joining the search teams.

Just before nightfall, I flipped from my stomach to my back and opened my Swiss Army knife. A knife blade made a primitive mirror, but it was good enough for me to see the blistering and burns on my cheeks. The cockpit fire had singed my eyebrows and eyelashes as well. At the time of the explosion I'd thought half my face had melted away. I had gotten off lucky.

As the sky slowly darkened, I was about to experience one of the greatest frustrations of my ordeal. I wanted to move as quickly as possible—hoof it all the way to the Adriatic Sea and find a boat back to Italy, if necessary. But because I was surrounded by hostile forces, I knew I had to move in slow motion. One jerky movement, one careless act of littering, one broken twig—any of those could give me away in an instant. I needed to be aware of my every movement, think several steps in advance, then check for errors once I'd made a move.

I knew from my survival training that night was the best time to travel. Even so, my safety wasn't guaranteed. Maybe the Serbs were stationed around the woods or had night vision goggles. I was particularly nervous about making any unnecessary noise, which can be heard farther away at night than in daytime. If I had to redesign the air force's survival vest, I would eliminate all Velcro.

No matter how carefully I opened a pocket of my vest, you could hear the sound halfway to China.

The air was cooling rapidly now. With regret I remembered the flight jacket I'd left hanging in my locker. I was getting hungry, too, and wished that lunch had been more than a few bites of pizza. To lift my spirits, I touched the little silver cross around my neck. It was an unusual and beautiful piece of jewelry—a small dove perched in the middle of a cross. My sister, Stacy, had given it to me as a present when I finished pilot training. I considered the cross a symbol of my faith and never took it off my neck. Closing my eyes, I said another prayer, asking God to get me through these difficult times. Somehow, I knew He would. Nothing could have been worse than the last six hours. If He had spared me from harm so far, my faith told me He would continue to keep me safe.

I usually carried a medal of St. Christopher—the patron saint of travelers—in my flight suit pocket, but I'd left that in my locker, too, along with my wallet. I glanced down at the Rolex watch, the present from my father. I knew what would happen if I was captured. The Rolex would be gone in a wink . . . a nice little war souvenir for somebody. I was determined that would never happen. Nobody was going to capture me.

I began to think of my goals. The first was to survive.

The second was to evade the enemy. The third was to make radio contact and get myself rescued. I knew that survival didn't always mean evading the enemy. If you were seriously hurt and were going to die without prompt medical attention, it was your duty to turn yourself over to your enemy if that was the only person who could care for you. You owed it to yourself and your nation to survive. When you were healthy again, then you would try to escape.

But I *was* healthy, and I was determined to evade the enemy. I remembered the motto of our Thirty-first Fighter Wing at Aviano. The Thirty-first was a proud group, with a remarkable history of wars and battles to its credit, including many stories of prisoners of war. The motto of the Thirty-first was simple and, in my circumstances, straight to the point. They were the words written on our insignia shield, just under the winged dragon: "Return with Honor." That was exactly what I intended to do.

Midnight passed before I finally made my move. There was no moon and only a handful of stars. A dark night. *Good for avoiding the enemy*, I thought. *Not so good for navigating*. Slowly and quietly, I slipped out of my harness, and along with the Ziploc bag that had held my radio, I left everything in a pile. The locals would easily find the gear, but by then I would be long gone. This would be the only time I would leave anything behind, even the smallest piece of trash. I kept on my G suit for the little extra warmth it provided.

I made a mental checklist of what I had left. Then I tried to stand. An act I normally took for granted was suddenly almost impossible. First, I was incredibly stiff from lying so long in the same position. Second, I had to move in superslow motion. It took me five minutes to push up my torso with my right hand, then pivot to a sitting position. Feeling every muscle in my body, and aching in most of them, I advanced to a squat and finally to my feet. Between each movement I stopped and listened for soldiers or civilians. The night was as quiet as a church. Picking up my survival rucksack as though it were a football, I baby-stepped out of the woods and into the grass.

It had taken me almost an entire hour to leave my hiding place. I was feeling weak and light-headed, and after a while I was trembling from the cold. Listening to my own rough breathing, I could see dim shapes eight or ten feet ahead of me. Everything was a fuzzy shade of gray, and I moved with caution.

I tried one direction, hit a dead end of dense trees, then took another route. It was almost like being blindfolded. Heading south from my landing site, I eventually found a narrow path that took me up an incline and into a grassy cove of tall, willowy trees. It was another dead end, but as good a place as any to hide for the next twenty-four hours. In my state of exhaustion, I was ready to crash. I had been traveling for more than three hours and had probably covered less than half a mile.

I stepped into a nearby clearing and opened my rucksack to see what it contained. I might have lost my flashlight, but I had a penlight in the shoulder pocket of my flight suit. Its white beam seemed brighter than the sun. Afraid of being seen, I dared using the light only once or twice, and for the briefest of seconds. In my rucksack I found eight small containers, called flexipaks, of water. This was about a quart of water in total. I also had an empty plastic water pouch, a gray wool ski hood, a yellow sponge, a pair of green wool socks and a pair of wool mittens, a floppy orange hat, a tarp that was green on one side and silver on the other, a large square of camouflage netting, a silver-foil space blanket, sun goggles and sunblock lotion, a fire starter, a five-inch knife, and a 121-page booklet titled *Aircrew Survival.*

If I found any humor in my situation, the thought of reading *Aircrew Survival* was it. When you're trying to avoid being captured, you don't have the time to sit around and read a book the way you would in a library. The other items in the rucksack had different degrees of usefulness to me. Since I was trying to hide from the enemy, I had serious doubts about the floppy orange hat and the sun-reflecting space blanket. Stuck in the damp cold of the mountains, however, I found the wool socks and mittens a godsend. Some items I had in my survival vest were also of value: a compass, a medical kit, iodine tablets to purify dirty water, rescue flares, camouflage paste, a tourniquet to stop the bleeding in case I got hurt, and most important, my battery-operated GPS navigational receiver. I had a 9-mm Beretta pistol in my holster, but it would have been foolish to use it. The enemy had had me outgunned from the moment they'd shot down my plane.

I donned the fresh pair of wool socks as well as the ski mask for warmth, and took out my GPS. Next to my radio, the GPS receiver was my most critical piece of equipment. It, too, operated on batteries, and I had to be careful not to run them down. The size of a Walkman, with a liquid crystal display screen, the GPS could calculate my longitude and latitude within 100 feet of my exact location. It did this by picking up the signals of at least three separate satellites, then triangulating, or fixing, my position on the ground.

Impatiently, I turned on my GPS receiver and waited. It seemed forever before the screen indicated that the first satellite had been found. After fifteen agonizing minutes, I had my three satellites in line, and the readout indicated my longitude and latitude. My spirits improved. Now I could communicate to somebody where I was. I brought out my radio and turned to the Guard frequency. Again, I knew the risk of my signal's being picked up by Serbs, but I also wanted the greatest chance of being rescued. Maybe, I hoped, there was a pair of friendly ears in the sky.

"Anyone, Basher Five-Two," I called.

With a heavy heart I listened to the crisp sound of static.

"Anyone, Basher Five-Two," I repeated.

More static. I tried not to feel discouraged. The radio worked by line-of-sight contact. At night, I had no idea what the landscape around me was like. If a mountain I couldn't see was in the way, the signal wouldn't go anywhere. I thought how great it would be if I had a different type of radio—one that was satellite based, like my GPS, with virtually unlimited range and secured channels. I planned to try my radio again in a few hours. If I still couldn't get any reception, I'd find a clear and secure place for sending my signal tomorrow.

I put the radio and the GPS receiver away, zipped up my rucksack, and nestled into my new hiding place in the cove. I was exhausted but much too pumped up for sleep. It would be light in a few hours. All I could do was wait to see what the day would bring and thank God that I was still alive.

SIX

With the first light of dawn, I got a rude surprise. I was lying peacefully in the darkness on my tarp, the green side folded over me, with the camouflage netting spread on top. Even though my feet and head stuck out of the netting, I had thought the trees concealed me well. I had opened a flexipak and had taken my first drink of water in seventeen hours. Just as I was congratulating myself on fooling the enemy, I realized I wasn't concealed at all.

The night had tricked me. The thick trees that by touch and through my dim sight had seemed so perfect had, in fact, very few low branches. I would stick out like an elephant to anyone coming up the path. I tried not to panic. Ever so slowly, I gathered my gear and slipped toward the clearing where I'd made my radio transmissions. Not far away, amid a stand of skinny trees, there were low branches I could hide under. And if I had to flee, I wasn't trapped in a total dead end. I picked a hiding spot and prepared to burrow in.

Several years before, I had taken a two-week survival course at Fairchild Air Force Base in Spokane and, later, a one-week water survival course at Holmstead Air Force

Base. I had learned tons of useful things in both courses, but the training at Fairchild was the most relevant now. My instructors had emphasized the importance of finding a good hiding spot, or "hole-up" site, as the military called it. A hole-up site was only good if you followed the BLISS principle. Your hole had to *b*lend into the environment. It had to be *l*ow and regular *i*n *s*hape. And it had to be in a *s*ecluded area. It was also helpful if you had some protection from the elements, a way to escape when cornered, an ability to see the land around you, and clear radio reception. By itself each part was minor, but if you followed them all, they could add up to the difference between success and failure.

With my new hole I wasn't batting a thousand, but as I set up my tarp and netting at a nerve-rackingly slow pace, I felt I was doing well under the circumstances. When I was finally settled in, I pulled my evasion chart from my G-suit pocket and began to plot the longitude and latitude coordinates I'd gotten from my GPS receiver last night.

My evasion chart, known as EVC—the military has initials for everything—was basically a topographical map of Bosnia. It showed all the hills, valleys, rivers, and land features around me. On its legend was other helpful information about local vegetation and animals, including a poisonous snake called the European viper. I wanted to be sure to avoid that. For all its usefulness, however, the

EVC had two major disadvantages. First, it was made of a heavy-duty, waterproof material that you couldn't fold or unfold without waking the dead. Second, because the EVC was designed to serve in emergencies as a blanket or a splint or even a tarp for hauling supplies, it was huge— almost five feet by three feet. I used my knife to cut out the piece of the EVC that showed my immediate area, and I shoved the rest into my rucksack. Once I'd plotted my coordinates on my new, smaller EVC, I picked out a hill about two miles away that I hoped would make a decent stage for a rescue attempt. As I would be moving only at night, two miles was a lot of territory to cover, but reaching that hill became my new goal.

Setting goals was a necessity for me. Whether it was to grab a quick nap, find something to eat, or move a few yards closer to that final hill, having a goal focused my thoughts and energies. Growing up, I had always carved out one goal or another for myself. Whether it was making my high-school football team or becoming an air force pilot or getting rescued, I could never live my life any other way.

Lying there in that hole, I would at times grow sad and feel sorry for myself. That's when I tried my best to remember that I had been extremely lucky so far. I knew the Vietnam-era stories of U.S. Navy and Air Force pilots who'd been shot down by the enemy and captured and who had then spent years in captivity. Many had died. If

66

I was captured in the days ahead, I too had to be prepared to give my life for my country. I knew I could do that, but I also knew that if I stayed alert and determined, the enemy would have to be very good and very lucky to find me. During the Vietnam conflict, an American pilot named Lance Sijan had been forced to eject from his plane over the mountains of Laos. His leg was mangled, and with no emergency rucksack containing water or food, he had to crawl through the Laotian jungle for six weeks, surviving on whatever he could find. Later he was captured, managed to escape, but was recaptured by the enemy. Eventually he died in a prison in Hanoi. Nevertheless, his strong will to survive and be free was an inspiration to every pilot I knew.

Staring out at the Bosnian countryside, I began to wonder what was happening at Aviano. I knew it was too early to assemble any kind of rescue attempt. No one had proof that I was alive or knew where I was. But I was confident that I hadn't been forgotten. I hoped that Wilbur and other pilots were flying overhead looking and listening for some sign of me. My friends weren't going to let me down, just as I wouldn't have let them down if they had been in my shoes. Teamwork is the cornerstone of the military. From the first day of your training you learn to trust and rely on the person next to you, just as he or she trusts and relies on you.

In the middle of my thoughts, I suddenly heard two

male voices in the distance. I immediately pressed as deeply as I could into the ground. The voices grew clearer and louder. Soon I could hear footsteps. Where had they come from? Were they soldiers? I curled my body into a tight ball and once more held my breath. I was staring into the ground and couldn't see their faces. Though I wore my gray ski mask, I didn't risk looking up. I knew from survival school that just the whites of your eyes were enough to give you away.

The two men came within feet of me—as close as the grandfather and grandson had come yesterday—and, miraculously, they walked on.

I don't know how long I waited before I turned my head and gazed back at the countryside. Everything looked peaceful, but my ears told me a different story. I could hear gunfire in the distance, and after a few hours the rotor blades of a helicopter vibrated in the sky. The chopper was skimming the tree line and for a few seconds hovered nearby. My heart leaped to my throat. Could it be from Aviano? I twisted my head up and recognized a Soviet-made chopper called the Gazelle. The chopper belonged to my enemy, not to any of my rescuers. I could actually pick out the faces of the two pilots, and even though I was well hidden, I worried about their spotting me by chance. The fact that the Serbs were now mounting an air search meant that I was a very valuable prize. More soldiers and helicopters would probably be coming.

Minutes earlier, I had boldly thought of trying to make radio contact during daylight. The sight of the Gazelle chopper convinced me to give up that fantasy. I couldn't risk having my signal intercepted by the enemy and being found.

There were no more incidents the rest of the day. I could hear cows mooing in the distance, but no sounds of people. By evening I was prepared to move again. My goal was to make my way toward that hill I had marked on my EVC. I didn't know how long it would take, and I wasn't going to fix a deadline. I was mentally prepared to be in Bosnia for weeks, if necessary, because I refused to rush into careless mistakes.

Sometime around nightfall I made the decision not to pick up and run. Despite the encounter with the two men this morning, my hole-up site gave me decent cover, and I wasn't risking too much by sticking around another twenty-four hours. There might also be something to gain. First, I needed to conserve and even build my strength. If I got some sleep, I'd be in better shape for tomorrow night's journey. I hadn't slept in thirty-six hours. Why struggle ahead now, when my mind wasn't clear? Second, I'd have ample time tonight to try my radio again. Third, I could keep observing and listening to what was around me. I could do some intelligence gathering and maybe pick up a pattern of enemy activity.

The night went by peacefully. I tried my radio two or

three times in the nearby clearing but heard only the familiar pattern of static. I took several short "combat naps." These are fitful rests at best, during which you're just on the edge of unconsciousness, ready to wake at the slightest noise. Dawn finally came, damp and chilly. I kept my arms close to my torso, hugging myself to keep warm. Even though this was summer, the mountainous climate made for cold nights and gray, drizzly days.

I also woke up hungry. When it came to survival, I knew that food was not nearly as important as water or even sleep. You could live weeks without eating, but not more than a week without some kind of liquid. Go even three days without water, my instructors had told me, and your thinking would become unreliable. But I wasn't terribly worried about water at the moment. I still had most of my flexipaks, and from the dark clouds that had gathered yesterday evening, I guessed there would be rain soon. Mostly I was just hungry.

I hadn't spotted any fruit or berries in the woods. Boldly, I picked a leaf off a tree that I couldn't identify. Oval, pointed at one end, and thin, the leaf looked harmless enough. Before you stick anything strange into your mouth, you are supposed to test it for harmful effects. The first step is to rub the plant or leaf on the outside of your lip. If your lip becomes irritated, the leaf is no good to eat. If there is no irritation, you rub the leaf on the

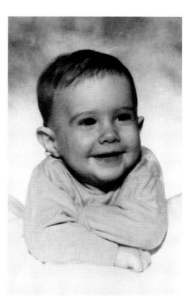

Here I am, only a few months old. *(Courtesy of Mary Lou Scardapane)*

I've always enjoyed doing things with my dad. I learned a lot from him about the importance of working hard and taking pride in whatever I did. My dog's name was Pepsi. *(Courtesy of Mary Lou Scardapane)*

When I was four years old, my family lived in New York City. One year I was Batman for Halloween. That's my sister, Stacy, beside me. *(Courtesy of Mary Lou Scardapane)*

Christmas 1971 with my mom, my brother, Paul, and my sister, Stacy. *(Courtesy of William O'Grady)*

My first horse ride, at age six, on Brownie at Joe's Stables in California. *(Courtesy of William O'Grady)*

In Cub Scouts, I really enjoyed learning about animals, nature, and wilderness survival. *(Courtesy of William O'Grady)*

We moved to Spokane, Washington, when I was nine. I'm the kid in the middle. *(Courtesy of Mary Lou Scardapane)*

When I was ten, I began skiing. Here I am at Mount Spokane with my sister. *(Courtesy of William O'Grady)*

In the F-16 with the bubble canopy up. *(Courtesy of William O'Grady)*

The official patch
of my squadron.
(Courtesy of the author)

The cockpit of the F-16. *(Courtesy of Lockheed Martin Tactical Aircraft Systems)*

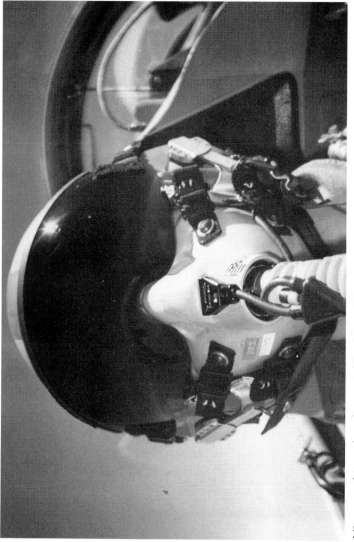

All strapped in and ready to go! That's how I look wearing the helmet and oxygen mask. *(Courtesy of Mary Scardapane)*

The F-16 in flight. (*Courtesy of Lockheed Martin Tactical Aircraft Systems*)

The Super Cobras and Super Stallions as they lift off from the deck of the USS *Kearsarge* to carry out their TRAP mission to rescue me. *(Courtesy of USMC Sergeant Dave A. Garten)*

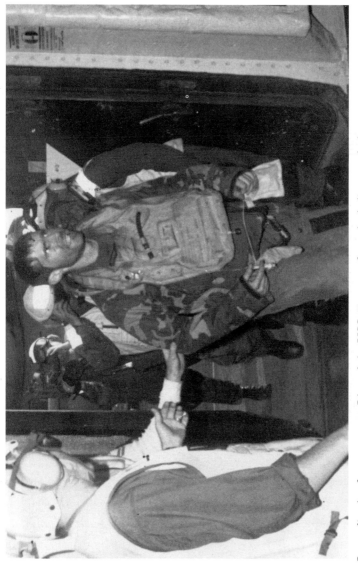

Immediately after my rescue, I board the USS *Kearsarge* from the helicopter deck. *(Courtesy of USMC)*

The men who rescued me and lifted me out of Bosnia—the members of the 24th Marine Expeditionary Unit who participated in the TRAP mission. Their mission completed, they clean their weapons aboard the USS *Kearsarge*. *(Courtesy of USMA Corporal Kurt Sutton)*

A group portrait of my rescue team posed before a Super Stallion. *(Courtesy of U.S. Department of Defense)*

I give the Juvats sign upon arriving at the Aviano NATO air base. *(Courtesy of AP/World Wide Photos)*

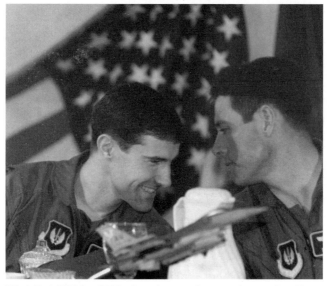

With Bob "Wilbur" Wright, who was flying with me when I was shot down. *(Courtesy of AP/Wide World Photos)*

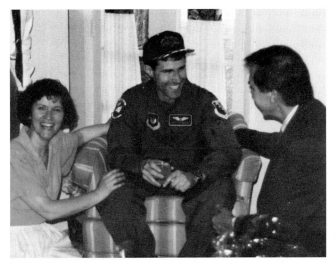

One very happy return. At Andrews Air Force Base with my mom and dad. *(Courtesy of Mary Lou Scardapane)*

Reunited with my family . . . at the White House! *(Courtesy of Mary Lou Scardapane)*

Taking a stroll with my commander in chief, President Clinton, at the White House. *(Courtesy of AP/World Wide Photos)*

inside of your lip, to see if that causes a reaction. If not, the next step is to put it in your mouth for a few minutes. If there is no burning, itching, or nausea, you can swallow it with some confidence.

Taking the recommended time between each step, you could spend up to four hours just waiting to swallow your first leaf. I didn't feel so patient. After dining on my first piece of greenery, I waited a full hour, felt no ill effects, and swallowed several more leaves. I tried to pick clean ones, without any spots or marks. They had no real taste, and my mouth felt terribly dry afterward. Rather than fill my stomach, the leaves simply made me thirsty. For the rest of the morning I downed the water in several of the flexipaks, including two within a thirty-minute period. Even under normal circumstances the body requires about two quarts a day; with stress, you are supposed to drink more. What little I had, I did my best to enjoy. Each sip tasted more glorious than the freshest glass of orange juice. I kept looking up to the sky, praying for rain. By late afternoon a few drops had landed on my face. Then the sky closed like a door.

Throughout the day I heard cowbells, and I worried that a herd and its handler might be coming my way. The Soviet-made helicopter made another pass above me before drifting on. Several times I turned on my radio, fitting in my earpiece snugly so that no sound could escape. There was little to hear besides static. Was the radio broken or the batteries not strong enough? Or was I just out of transmission range?

My morale worsened by the end of the day. I wondered if the lack of water was starting to affect my judgment. Had I wasted a whole day here? Was I really strong enough to move on tonight? Doubts about being rescued dampened my mood. I closed my eyes and said another prayer, a special one this time, inspired by the very country in which I was now so hopelessly lost. The previous winter, when I was in the States for training, I had visited a friend of my mom's. Her name was Anita, and she'd just come back from the town of Medjugorje, in the south of Bosnia, where many locals and visitors had sworn they'd seen the Virgin Mary. I had never believed in miracles, but I suddenly found myself praying to the Mother of Medjugorje. I began to feel an inner peace, a certainty that I wasn't alone in the world. I felt that a lot of people were praying for me and my safe return. It was almost like a chorus of voices, and it renewed my courage.

Late that night, I rose stiffly from my hiding place with slow, disconnected movements. My goal was not to disturb a single twig as I pushed to my feet. Once again, I checked off the items in my rucksack and made sure my radio was secure in my survival vest pocket. I plugged in the earpiece so that I could listen to the radio as I walked. In between my vest and my flight suit I stuffed my tarp, the netting, and the large portions of my EVC, until I looked as though I were several months pregnant. I carried my rucksack like a backpack. I stepped into the meadow and began traveling southeast, heading toward the hill I had indicated on my evasion chart.

My day of rest in the woods had not been wasted. While I was still thirsty and hungry, I felt a new reserve of energy. Although there were more stars out than last night, making me more noticeable to any sleepless Serbs, I looked upon the night as an old and reliable friend. My legs pushed me up a hill, over its crest, and into an open field. I hesitated. The thought of being exposed as I marched across the field worried me. It made more sense to take extra time and walk along the borders of the field, where there were trees to conceal me. Then I remembered the motto of the Juvats, the Eightieth Fighter Squadron, with whom I had served in Korea. *Audentes fortuna juvat,* I told myself. Fortune favors the bold. I began walking across the open field.

Maybe I suddenly had get-home-itis. The desire to get out of Bosnia *now* fought with the more cautious voice inside me, the one begging me to slow down and be careful. As I navigated across the field, my pace quickened along with my heart. After about fifteen minutes I came over a rise and stopped cold. A pair of steel power line towers, about a quarter mile apart, dominated the landscape like a couple of giants.

I began to worry about being near a population center. Worse, it was less than an hour before daylight. Birds were already starting to sing. As I hurried ahead, the field narrowed into a broad path, which led up a slope to some dense foliage. With the rucksack bouncing on my back, I sped up my pace toward what looked like a secluded cove, bordered by a steep six-foot-high granite ledge. Still in darkness, I dropped into a maze of bushes and trees.

Using the Guard channel, twice I called out on my radio. Even though I was now on higher ground, where the transmission should have been better, I got nowhere. Frustrated, I closed my eyes. I didn't mean to fall asleep, but I did. When I was awakened by the first light of dawn, it took me only seconds to realize I had made the same mistake as two nights ago. In my haste to hide and my inability to see clearly, I had chosen a less than desirable hole-up site. The trees and the undergrowth were too sparse. And the granite ledge behind me made a quick escape difficult.

As the sky flooded with light, I dashed ten yards into a clump of high thistle bushes across the way. I didn't care if the thistles scratched my face and hands; the important thing was that they were deep enough to cover me. I went through my slow-motion routine of laying down my tarp and covering myself with the camouflage netting, but not before spreading out my gear so that everything was within easy reach. I had a strict and specific place for each piece of my gear—penlight here, radio there, GPS receiver by my leg. I had come to think of setting up camp as building a nest. It was a step-by-step process, like that of a mother bird bringing in nest material straw by straw. The overall effort, considering how slowly and carefully the nest had to be built, was exhausting. Even stopping to go to the bathroom took ten times longer than normal. At the end of the nest building, my feet once again stuck out of the short netting, my boot heels resting only a few feet from the open field of grass. There was nothing I could do about it. My hole-up site wasn't perfect, but at least I could see the whole cove and the path leading into it.

Around me birds flitted from one tree branch to another. Earlier I'd seen a black squirrel scamper across the ground. As hungry as I was, there was no way I could catch the squirrel or a bird, much less start a fire to cook them. The distant sound of a jet to the south took my mind off my stomach. My neck arched up, and I scanned the skies eagerly, hoping the plane was one of ours. The clouds were too thick to see anything, but it didn't matter, I thought. My faith told me the plane *had* to be one of NATO's. It was now Monday. I had been shot down late Friday afternoon. No one had given up on me.

Fumbling with my radio, I tuned in and tried to monitor both the Guard and the Alpha channel. That's when I realized that part of my earpiece—the tiny nipple in the middle—was missing. My hands began desperately to search the ground around me. I couldn't silently monitor the radio without the entire earpiece. And what if the part had fallen on the path to the cove or in the larger meadow? That was the kind of mistake I had worked so hard to avoid. If a local found it, he or she would be sure to tell the entire world, and I could expect an invasion of soldiers. Twenty minutes later, the crisis was over; I found the missing part inside my tarp.

By the time I fitted in my earpiece, the skies had cleared of any jets. And my radio turned up nothing.

I used my GPS to ring in three satellites for a fresh set of coordinates. It was nice to know some piece of equipment was working. I was also thankful that I wasn't too far from my destination. I could make my chosen hill in another day—if I managed to stay alert and focused. My growing concern was water. I'd finished my last flexipak of water early that morning. In forty-eight hours I'd consumed a total of one quart, whereas my body had really needed a minimum of a gallon and a half. Every day the skies turned a deep, leaden gray, followed by a late afternoon or evening drizzle. But it was never enough rain to catch in a Ziploc bag. It was only enough to make me cold and damp. My EVC didn't show any nearby streams or creeks. While I could hear cows mooing in the background and knew they had to have a source of water, I wasn't ready to go exploring and risk running into a farmer.

I don't know how long I spent praying for a cloudburst. It didn't have to be the size of Noah's flood, I told God, just enough to help me fill my very dry body. My mind kept drifting, and though I tried to stay alert, I fell asleep.

A sharp, repeated clanging woke me. I had been sleeping for maybe thirty minutes. As I struggled awake, the ground trembled behind me, and I was afraid that I had been discovered. Instead, crashing down around me were not soldiers but a pair of large cows. The clanging came from their handler, a man or woman ringing a loud bell, somewhere behind them and out of sight. I thought of shooing the cows away, but that might draw the attention of their handler. My new friends settled in by the grass next to my thistle patch and began munching away to their heart's content, scarcely looking up at me.

To amuse myself, I named the two cows Alfred and Leroy, even if those were boys' names and cows are female. They were the first names that popped into my head. I called their handler Tinker Bell because he or she wouldn't stop ringing the bell. In one sense I liked the noise. I always knew where Tinker Bell was because of the ringing. But after a while the constant ringing drove me crazy. As the afternoon wore on, Leroy came up to my boots as they peeked through the camouflage netting.

I kept looking over my shoulder, wondering if cows liked leather. But my clothes were of much less interest to Leroy and Alfred than were the strands of juicy grass. After a while my friends had had their fill and wandered back the way they'd come. I never did see Tinker Bell.

During Monday night it rained. Not just another frustrating drizzle, but a hard, merciless thunderstorm that soaked everything around me. At first I just turned on my back and opened my mouth, catching every drop I could. Soon I was using my yellow sponge, frantically running it over the crevices of my rucksack, soaking up the small pools of water. I squeezed out the sponge into a Ziploc bag, overjoyed as I watched the level steadily rise before me. I sponged water off my tarp, my vest, any surface that would cooperate. I didn't have to worry about making too much noise or jerky movements—because no one else was going to be out in this storm. When the rain stopped an hour later, I'd added another pint of water to my travel pouch and had drunk enough to stop the burning in my throat.

As the storm front passed, the night sky lit up with brilliant clusters of stars. Two meteors streaked across the heavens with a beauty I couldn't describe. I was reminded of my summers at Camp Reed and the clear skies of northeastern Washington. I thought of my family and friends back home. Were they seeing the same stars I was watching tonight? The nostalgia hit me hard.

When I came out of my daze, I realized that if I was ever to get home, instead of just dreaming about it, I had to try something different from what I had been doing. I pulled out my radio and turned to the Guard channel. Instead of transmitting my voice, which had gotten me nowhere the last three days, I turned on the universal distress beacon. This was a high-pitched alarm, and for a radio operator it was certainly easier to understand than was a garbled human voice. As the alarm went out, I monitored the radio for a response, turning from Guard to Alpha, the channel with the most privacy, and back to Guard. Nothing. If somebody was listening, they didn't let me know it.

I waited ten minutes and tried the beacon again. At first, moving back and forth between Guard and Alpha, I heard only familiar static. A minute later, on the Guard channel, a faint voice broke through. In English, no less. It was a bigger surprise than making contact with ET, and sweeter than a Garth Brooks melody. My heart was about to explode. I pushed the earpiece snugly into my ear and listened intently.

"Flashman, this is Magic on Guard . . . heard some beacons . . . see if you can—"

My mind sped ahead. Who was Flashman? Some pilot, I guessed, maybe on temporary duty at Aviano or some other NATO base in Europe. I knew Magic was NATO's airborne command post. Maybe Magic had heard me. A moment later came a second, equally faint voice.

"Basher Five-Two, this is Flashman . . . hear me."

I shut my eyes. Flashman was looking for *me*. Before I could respond, the mysterious pilot spoke again. "Basher Five-Two, this is Flashman on Guard, if you hear me."

I gripped the radio so tightly I thought it might shatter. *"Flashman, this is Basher Five-Two,"* I almost screamed.

"Basher Five-Two, this is Flashman, if you hear me, on Guard."

He couldn't hear me! Controlling myself, I gave my call sign slowly and clearly. Again, there was no response. I kept waiting.

"Anybody," I finally said. *"Basher Five-Two."*

Flashman had gone. I sat back down on the ground. My emotions were mixed. I was badly disappointed that Flashman hadn't received my transmission, but I was overjoyed that my radio was working and that NATO was looking for me. I was right, I had not been forgotten. Flashman, or somebody else, would be back. With my radio finally in receiving range of their messages, I knew I would be in contact again.

My mother, after the visit from the chaplain and other air force officers to her Seattle home, immediately called my sister, Stacy. An eighth-grade public school teacher in

Chicago, Stacy took the news harder than anybody else. Unlike my mom, who refused to believe I was dead, Stacy assumed the worst. She had never really liked my flying an F-16 because she considered it extremely dangerous. Growing up as the older brother, I had always protected her. Once I became a fighter pilot, she thought that somehow she had to protect me. She had given me the cross with the dove—so that I would always know she was thinking of me, she said—and whenever we got together she wanted to be reassured that I was the most safety-conscious pilot in the world. Now, when she received the bad news at her Chicago school, she felt a grief that not even her friends or my mother could assuage.

Sharing the same birth date, Stacy and I also shared a special brother-sister intuition, and she knew I would want her to be with my parents during this terrible time. Stacy talked with my mom, and they agreed that it was my dad, living on the other coast in Virginia, who most needed her support. Stacy flew out the next day to be with him. My brother, Paul, joined them a day later, on Sunday. At Dad's house they constantly watched news channels and tried to rally each other's spirits. As long as the Serbs didn't report finding my body, there was hope. The same afternoon that Paul arrived, the Serbs reported that they had captured me. The news was greeted with shouts of joy and calls to other relatives across the nation. At least if I had been captured, the theory went, I was alive. The Serbs wouldn't dare hurt a NATO peace-keeper, would they?

The Serbs had no evidence to show the world that I was their prisoner. All they had was video footage of the twisted wreckage of my F-16. Shown on Western news channels, the pictures looked grim. Everyone in my family wondered how any pilot could have survived a missile strike. When no fresh news followed about me, hope gave way to despair. Experts on television expressed doubts that the Bosnian Serbs were telling the truth about finding me. Colonel Charles Wald, commander of the Thirty-first Fighter Wing at Aviano, called my dad and mom to tell them that NATO was doing everything possible to find me. Still, he didn't provide them with any specific plan. My dad hoped that, for military security reasons, Colonel Wald simply wouldn't reveal that *some* rescue attempt was afoot. By late Sunday night, my family could only sit around and wait and worry—just like me, 12,000 miles away.

On Monday, another colonel called to tell my family that a mysterious beacon signal had been picked up in the area where I'd been shot down and that the U.S. Air Force also had unconfirmed reports of a parachute sighting. My family's spirits lifted again, until they were warned that without voice communication to back up the beacon, this could all be a trick of the Bosnian Serbs.

On Tuesday the Serbs told Western journalists that I

had never been captured and admitted they had no idea whether I was alive or dead.

My dad clung to the hope that if I had parachuted out of my plane, I was still alive. He knew of all the practice jumps I'd taken at Fort Benning, and like everything else I'd pursued in my life, he knew how much effort I'd put into my training. But Stacy was less optimistic. She would stand in Dad's backyard and stare blankly at the sky. The only hope she felt came from that special bond between us, the one that we kept in our hearts. She thought of the cross necklace she had given to me as a present. As long as I wore *that*, she told herself, I was going to be okay.

SEVEN

Somewhere between Monday night and Tuesday morning I was awakened from a combat nap by an explosion that shook the ground around me. Confused and frightened, I was in fear for my life and wanted to dig myself deeper into my hole-up site. The strange explosion was followed by a tomblike silence. A mortar, a hand grenade, an artillery shell, maybe even a sonic boom from a jet—it could have been anything. All I knew for sure was that the hole-up site wasn't as safe as I'd hoped.

I considered repacking everything in my rucksack and moving instantly, but with the birds already chirping away, I knew it was close to sunrise. I would have to stay low for another eighteen hours, try to get some rest, and under darkness plod on toward the hill I'd chosen for my rescue site.

After the mysterious boom, though exhausted, I was too on edge to sleep. I turned on my radio and kept monitoring it in vain. I wondered if Leroy and Alfred would return, with Tinker Bell in tow. I worried, too, about a condition called hypothermia, in which your core body temperature drops dangerously below the normal temperature of 98.6 degrees Fahrenheit. If this happens, your mind becomes confused. I worried that this might influence me to make bad decisions that could lead to my capture. After the last rain, my clothes were still wet, and in addition to the normal damp cold, I was shivering badly. Even though I was wearing my mittens and ski mask to prevent heat loss from my body, I would have given anything to start a roaring bonfire.

My mind was continually reeling in one direction or another. Besides praying to God and trusting that my family hadn't given up hope, I thought about all my buddies in the air force. I had made so many friends over the years. The deepest friendships had come during my one-year tour with the Eightieth Fighter Squadron, or the Juvats, at Kunsan Air Base in South Korea. There, married officers weren't allowed to bring their families. Pilots worked and lived together twenty-four hours a day. When we weren't flying sorties near the border between South and North Korea, we took our meals together, shared thoughts and emotions, and partied hard in our time off. Like a special club or fraternity, we Juvats had our slogans, hand gestures, songs, and traditions. We were forever making toasts and giving speeches, which I kept brief because I wasn't much for public speaking. And, of course, a Juvat pilot never could forget the Juvat salute—two fists raised high above the head and facing each other.

In March 1993, I had been reassigned to a fighter

squadron in Germany, and a year after that, to Aviano, but I would never forget Kunsan and my fellow Juvats. That was the year that *trust* and *loyalty* acquired an even deeper meaning for me. If you were a fighter pilot, ready to give your life for your country at any moment, you needed strong personal bonds with those around you, a belief that you were never alone. Teamwork meant that if you had to, you would sacrifice yourself for your fellow pilots, and they for you.

As the morning passed, I monitored my radio without picking up any voices, just more dull static. I told myself that reception would be better at night, and in any case I would be free to talk into the radio. Throughout the day my mood constantly shifted, between hope that I would be rescued at any minute and despair that I would be stranded in Bosnia for weeks or even months. My feelings were not caused by any lack of faith in God or my fellow pilots. I was just afraid of getting my hopes up and then being disappointed. I needed to think carefully— and not just expect to be rescued soon. Self-reliance was something I'd learned at an early age, and my military training had emphasized it, too. I had also learned from my dad that if one solution didn't work, you had to be creative and try another.

At the moment, although I was not particularly hungry, my most pressing need was keeping up my strength. If I was going to be running for cover every night, week after week, I had to fill my stomach. Glancing around, I snatched a couple of leaves from a tree, gave them my is-it-safe-to-eat test, and had the same reaction as before. The leaves were incredibly dry and only made me thirsty. I was wondering what else I could gobble up when my gaze was attracted to something moving in front of me.

Strolling next to my hand was a thin brown ant. I watched him head off to join his fellow ants, which, about three feet beyond, were happily feasting on a dead worm. I watched the scene with interest. I had never eaten ants, despite encouragement from more than one survival instructor. The very idea of eating bugs made me faintly sick. But circumstances change, and I found myself squirming toward the decaying worm. I reached out with my mittened hand and plucked one poor ant out of the group, squishing him between my fist and my ruck-sack. I dropped him down the hatch, crunched down on him, and pushed him to the back of my mouth. I held him there and waited two minutes for a reaction. When I felt no irritation, I swallowed him whole.

I knew ants are high in fat and have more protein than even beef. They are also full of vitamins and minerals. In some places in Africa, ants can be as sweet as honey and are a popular treat. My meal of one ant was as sour as a lemon drop. Still, he didn't leave my mouth dry. I reached over and grabbed another ant. The group, sens-ing something was amiss, began scattering in all directions, but none was as quick or as determined as I. Within thirty minutes, I had made a meal of fifteen of them.

That afternoon, I heard another jet to the south but heard nothing on my radio. Besides my normal frustration, I began to worry again about wearing down my batteries. Unless something drastic and unexpected happened, I decided I would save my radio for later. Everything had to be in order, ready for my push toward that hill. Even though my ski mask covered most of my head, on my face and neck I put some green and brown camouflage paste, just to be extra careful. I put my survival gear back into the rucksack and into my vest, checking everything twice. Just when I was feeling mentally comfortable and was trying to rest before nightfall, I heard a familiar sound.

The heavy, dull clomping of hooves was slowly coming my way, along with that irritating clanging bell. I dropped flat on my tarp, thinking, *Here come Alfred and Leroy to their favorite dining spot.* Just as before, they began grazing within feet of me. Then up the path strolled Tinker Bell. From the loudness of his or her bell I knew Tinker Bell was closer than yesterday. I never did catch a glimpse of the cow herder, but what I feared most was that he or she might spot me. As long as that bell kept ringing, I knew Tinker Bell wasn't running off to tell his or her family or the local authorities.

After half an hour, the two cows and their handler disappeared. I had been saying prayers the whole time. Now I had the luxury of taking a deep breath and wondering what lay ahead.

It was close to midnight before I began my journey. Moving out of the thistle patch, loaded down with gear, I stumbled often, clumsily breaking twigs right and left. I worried about losing my balance and coordination. This could have been the result of hypothermia or another condition called dehydration, which is caused by the body's not receiving enough fluid. I finally found my way east, onto small flat fields bordered by bushy trees. I tried monitoring my radio as I moved, hoping to hear from Flashman, but it took my attention away from my path. The terrain was tricky, with swells and dips, and low rock walls that I had to climb over. After scaling one, I landed in a deep, muddy puddle. Surprised, and angry with myself for getting my boots and socks wet, I muttered in disgust and tramped on.

Not stopping at that moment was one of the things I most regretted during my entire ordeal. I could easily have filled a water bag to the brim, popped in an iodine tablet to purify the water, and satisfied my body's all-important need for liquid. I'd already gone through most of the water I'd saved from the thundershower. By the time I realized my error, I was advancing into another field. I didn't want to retrace my steps because I was having enough difficulty going forward. Even though I had my compass out and generally knew where I was heading, the gray, clustered shapes of nearby hills were confusing. Which was the specific hilltop I'd picked out on my EVC? I couldn't find it.

I was tempted to pull out my GPS, but even if I learned my coordinates, I'd have to verify them on the map. That meant using my penlight to see, and I knew I shouldn't take that risk. Once more the urge to rush everything and make contact with NATO tonight was at war with the voice that warned me to go slow and not hurry into a mistake. As I zigzagged through fields and climbed over walls, my sense of caution won out. An hour before sunrise I began searching for a hole-up site. I chose a cluster of trees and bushes near a three-foot rock wall. The site looked promising. An open pasture lay on the other side. I couldn't imagine any reason cows would have to leave their favorite pasture and jump over a wall to visit me.

The first light of Wednesday was less than an hour away. By the time I settled in, satisfied but exhausted, I was ready for a quick nap. But not before I made up for last night's blunder. I couldn't quite forgive myself for leaving that puddle of muddy water without even taking a sip. Removing my shoes, I yanked off my wet socks and wrung them out, one by one, over an open Ziploc bag, catching every dirty drop that I could. The amount I collected wasn't much, and the water tasted bitter, but I wasn't complaining.

I fell asleep and had my first real dream since being shot out of the sky. I dreamed that I didn't have to hide anymore because NATO had arranged to pick me up and the locals were helping by giving me food, a shower, and a bed.

I woke with a start. It was a sweet dream, but it hurt me to think it wasn't true. I so badly wanted out of Bosnia. I checked my tarp, my netting, and the branches that covered me. I pored over my EVC. I was within one night's journey of the hill where I wanted to be. All I had to do was scout for a decent landing spot for a helicopter. And pray to God that someone would hear me on my radio.

In the middle of the night I heard distant rifle fire. I tried to ignore my jitters as I gathered my radio and set out to explore. Before leaving my hole-up site, I turned up a corner of my tarp—to the silver side—so that the moon could reflect off it and show me the way back. Walking along the edge of the woods, I moved uphill, gathering and eating grass along the way to keep up my strength.

After about fifty yards, I found a small clearing that seemed perfect for sending a radio beacon. The site wasn't big enough for a helicopter to land, but maybe they could hover above and drop me a safety line and pull me up. I didn't see the need to go any farther and risk getting into trouble. With almost a full moon to guide me, I set up my GPS receiver and was lucky to quickly ring up not three but *four* satellites to fix my coordinates. Then I plugged in my earpiece and monitored my radio.

Official SAR (search-and-rescue) procedure was that NATO was supposed to contact me, not the other way around. But I'd already sent out more than one beacon, and after my frustrating attempt to reach Flashman, the airwaves had been strangely silent. I couldn't keep *only* monitoring. I had to *talk* to someone. Otherwise they might never find me, no matter how hard they were trying. Turning to the Guard channel, I flipped on the high-pitched beacon and kept it on for what seemed like minutes but was really only seconds. If the enemy was going to pick up my signal, so be it. This felt like my only chance of getting rescued. I began monitoring for a response, first on Guard, then on Alpha. The waiting was nerve-racking. Eating more grass was my way of staying calm.

Please, Lord, I prayed, *let them find me tonight. At least let them know I'm alive.*

For an hour I sat on a rock in the clearing, shivering, trying to stay warm by rubbing my hands together, and going back and forth to my radio. Turning it on and off, I waited for the miracle of a human voice. Then, on Alpha channel, it came. Not a voice, not yet. But three very clear, sharp clicks. No matter how much my mind was drifting, I was sure of that noise. It was the sound a microphone or a radio makes. Someone was on the other end. Someone was trying to call me.

EIGHT

Within an hour after I had been shot down on Friday, a badly shaken Bob "Wilbur" Wright, my flight leader, had returned to Aviano with grim news for everyone in the Triple Nickel. After watching my plane get blown apart by a missile, he had neither seen a parachute in the sky nor heard any radio message from the ground. He had made several caps, combat air patrols, above the immediate area, following our SAR plan, before reluctantly assuming the worst. At Aviano, pilots and wives listened to the grim news but somehow hoped that I had pulled off the impossible and survived.

On Sunday, when the Bosnian Serbs claimed that they had captured me, among all the pilots at Aviano no one wanted to believe that message more than Wilbur. And after Wilbur came Captain Tom "T.O." Hanford, the weapons and tactics officer of the Triple Nickel. Hanford had been flying F-16s for seven years and had lost a number of pilot friends in air accidents. To make the record worse for him, I would have been the first lost in a combat situation. When the Bosnian Serbs later admitted that they had *not* captured me, Hanford feared that I had died as a prisoner of war and the Serbs were simply afraid to tell the world the truth. There was only the slimmest chance, Hanford now believed, that I was alive and on the run. The only way to know for sure was to keep looking for me.

Search-and-rescue planes went out in pairs every day from Aviano, as did the usual sorties of F-16s as part of Operation Deny Flight. Everyone was fearful of the SAM batteries that had shot down my plane. If the Serbs could get me, the SAMs could get them, too. Pilots were ordered to fly their missions "feet wet," along the coastline, which was out of the missiles' range. Better there than in the no-fly zone, where I'd been hit. But from Aviano and other NATO bases in Italy, secret "packages" were, in fact, flying "feet dry" over Bosnia, searching for me. "Packages" meant a fleet of maybe six planes at one time, which had plenty of firepower to knock out any SAMs, if necessary. "Feet dry" meant flying over land, as opposed to "feet wet," flying over water.

Even if I didn't know it, Flashman had been part of one of those secret packages. He and all the search-and-rescue teams had their radios continually turned to Guard or Alpha. They repeatedly called out to me and waited for some signal in return. There had been little to make them hopeful. Several beacon signals had been picked up in the countryside since Friday afternoon. However, the signals were judged by Magic, the NATO airborne command post, to be too far from my crash site to belong to me.

Late Wednesday night, June 7, Hanford and his wingman, Captain Clark Highstrete, were on a Deny Flight sortie north of their normal route and only seventy-five miles from my crash site. For two hours, starting around 11:00 P.M., Hanford had trained his radar on the no-fly zone, looking for bad guys. Nothing showed up. By 1:25 A.M., Thursday morning, their sortie over, Hanford and Highstrete were cleared by Magic to return to Aviano. Hanford wasn't really looking for me—that was the job of search-and-rescue pilots—but with nothing else going on, he asked Magic if he could stay in the skies a little longer. He had enough fuel for an extra forty minutes of flying, he said, and just maybe he would get lucky and find me. Magic gave him permission to fly an additional twenty minutes. While Highstrete monitored Magic's frequency, Hanford turned his radio to the Alpha search-and-rescue channel.

"This is Basher One-One," he called, still in a race-track pattern off the coast of Croatia. "Looking for Basher Five-Two."

There was no answer. Patiently, he kept trying. Around 1:40 A.M., something strange came over his headset. Having switched briefly to the Guard channel, Hanford heard an irregular static pattern that sounded as though it could be a very faint beacon.

Hanford was interrupted by his wingman on their interflight radio. Their twenty minutes was up, Highstrete said, and Magic wanted them to return to Aviano. Knowing he still had extra fuel, Hanford asked Magic for permission to stay out longer. He had heard *something* on Guard, he told them. With Magic's okay, Hanford went back to monitoring. The normal pattern of static returned. Disappointed, he moved his radio frequency to Alpha.

"Basher Five-Two, this is Basher One-One on Alpha."

Hanford kept calling, circling over the coastline, peering into the distant lights of Bosnia. Things looked peaceful from his darkened cockpit. He tried to imagine where I might be hiding, what my thoughts were, how I was attempting to communicate. Minutes later, Highstrete interrupted again. Magic was worried—it knew both pilots were low on fuel and wanted them back at the base *now*. In a stern voice, Hanford told Magic he was well aware of his fuel level, but he wanted more time. A fellow pilot was down there somewhere, and Hanford said he was going to keep looking until the last possible moment. Nervously, Magic backed off. Still in a racetrack pattern, Hanford repeated his call sign on Alpha.

"Basher Five-Two, this is Basher One-One on Alpha."

His eyes kept dancing to his fuel gauge. In another minute he would have to turn back to Aviano. The worst thing he could do was run his wingman, Highstrete, out of fuel. As Hanford listened intently through his headset, the faintest of voices suddenly broke through a haze of static.

"Basher One-One . . . Basher Five-Two."

The voice sounded weak and tired. Hanford didn't want to jump to conclusions. "This is Basher One-One," he said, speaking slowly. "I can barely hear you—say your call sign."

"Basher One-One . . . Basher Five-Two . . ."

Again, the voice was almost too faint to be heard. Hanford was unsure. "Understand you are Basher Five-Two," he said. "This is Basher One-One on Alpha."

The low-fuel warning sounded on Hanford's on-board computer. He ignored the warning, pushing his F-16 farther east to improve his radio reception. He was suddenly flying over the interior of Croatia, coming close to the range of known SAM batteries. Now Highstrete had to urge his flight leader to return to Aviano.

"Basher Five-Two, this is Basher One-One, say again," Hanford said into his radio, ignoring Highstrete for the moment.

Then Hanford heard it. As clear as a church bell. He almost jumped out of his skin.

"This is Basher Five-Two . . . read you loud and clear!"

"Basher One-One has you loud and clear!" Hanford roared back. His plane briefly circled west, out of range, but when he turned east again, the voice on the ground returned even stronger.

"This is Basher Five-Two, how do you hear?"

"Basher Five-Two," Hanford bellowed, "this is Basher One-One!"

"I'm alive, I'm alive!"

"Copy that!" Hanford said joyfully. Tears were welling up, and his voice was cracking. There was just one small doubt he had to overcome. Hanford had to be sure this was no Serb trick, no ambush to bring him into SAM range.

"What was your squadron in Korea?" Hanford asked. We were good enough friends for him to know the answer.

"Juvats—Juvats!"

"Copy that, you're *alive*!"

It was 2:08 A.M. Hanford was so shaken he had forgotten standard radio procedure. He also didn't identify who he was, and I didn't ask. Basher One-One wrote down the code I gave him for my coordinates. This was the same special code that Wilbur and I had agreed on in our preflight briefing. Basher One-One told me to turn off my radio to save my batteries. Using a special Alpha frequency, we agreed to communicate again in half an hour. As his F-16 turned away, out of monitoring range, he and Highstrete dashed back over the Adriatic on what fumes were left in their gas tanks. They would refuel at an airborne tanker and return to me as quickly as possible.

Hanford's thoughts jumped ahead to the next step. He had to get my coordinates relayed to NATO. But he was also feeling the joy of the moment. He knew there were going to be a lot of happy folks back home.

NINE

Hanford wasted no time in radioing Magic as well as Aviano intel that he had found me, alive, safe, and apparently in decent shape physically, considering my six days on the run. Word was quickly relayed to the Pentagon, as well as to NATO headquarters in Vicenza, Italy, where it was around 2 A.M. The NATO officers in Vicenza were startled. They had been sending French and British jets on secret sorties over Bosnia since my plane had been shot down, but like the regular search-and-rescue teams from Aviano, the pilots had found no evidence I was alive. With the unexpected news from Hanford, the Vicenza command jumped into action.

Even before I had been shot down, tensions in Bosnia had increased over the last few weeks. When the Bosnian Serbs had captured the 350 NATO military observers and made them prisoners of war, NATO had placed on alert the 24th United States Marine Expeditionary Unit, a crack troubleshooting team called up to handle tough situations around the world. Part of the 24th Expeditionary Unit was a forty-two-member TRAP force—*T*actical *R*ecovery *A*ircraft and *P*ersonnel. They were now stationed on the USS *Kearsarge,* an assault ship cruising in the Adriatic. Since June 2, the men on the *Kearsarge* had been on standby, ready to rescue me, if necessary.

But there were several important questions that had to be answered before any rescue effort was launched. The first question was, *when?* Dawn was only hours away. A daylight mission would be risky, the NATO commanders thought, because the Bosnian Serbs could easily spot a slow-moving helicopter. If NATO could be sure that I would be safe waiting until nightfall, wasn't it best to delay the rescue until dark? The second question was, who should make the rescue? Several commando groups, stationed at various places in Europe, could do the job as well as the TRAP force on the *Kearsarge*. Which group was the best prepared and could act most quickly? By 2:30 A.M. there was still a lot of talk. Nothing had been decided.

As much joy as "T.O." Hanford felt the instant I uttered the word *Juvats* over the radio, it was nothing compared with my own emotions. I hadn't even recognized Hanford's voice. All I knew was that one of the good guys had found me and that my chances of being rescued had just improved dramatically. At last, everyone would have proof that I was alive, and they had my coordinates, too. I wasn't sure whether I wanted to scream at the top of my lungs or cry or fall down and thank God.

From Basher One-One's tone, I realized that no one

had picked up my earlier beacon signals. I had had a lot of fears during those six days, but one of my greatest was that my family would never know what had happened to me. Now, at least, they'd be told I had not only survived the missile attack, but I'd avoided capture. I had done my duty. I had served my country with honor.

Basher One-One returned around 2:45 A.M., and we made contact on our special Alpha frequency. We were both concerned about Bosnian Serb intelligence. I was so close to freedom—by now my get-home-itis had struck like the flu—and I knew this was the time I was most likely to make stupid mistakes. I was also, perhaps, the most at risk. I remembered the gunfire in the night. The Bosnian Serbs could be closer than I knew.

Basher One-One asked how I was. When I told him that I was okay, he hesitated, then dealt me a blow that sent me staggering.

"Magic wants me to pass you the word," he said. *"Ma-ñana."*

Mañana. Tomorrow. I couldn't believe it. NATO wasn't going to send a rescue team until the next night! Maybe I should have told Basher One-One that I was half dead and that if someone didn't come right away, there might be no *mañana*.

"No," I shouted back into my radio. "Get me the heck out of here *now!*"

Basher One-One tried to calm me down. He explained

that NATO was assembling a rescue team, but there were risks to be considered. In my military mind, I understood perfectly. Rescue forces liked to work at night—with high-tech gear like night goggles. Darkness gave them an advantage over a less well-equipped enemy—and in about three hours it would be daylight in Bosnia. As much as I wanted out, I definitely didn't want to put my rescue team in needless danger. I didn't want a bunch of men dying just to save my life. Waiting another twenty hours might be necessary.

In my heart, however, I was not quite so sure. I wanted out now. With all my radio transmissions, I worried that the enemy had surely heard me, and if I wasn't rescued right away, the Serbs would find me. I had used up enough of my nine lives surviving the last six days. I couldn't afford to chance another twenty hours.

Basher One-One promised to call me back, and again I turned off my radio. My batteries were growing weaker. Transmissions with Basher One-One were so faint that many times we had to repeat ourselves. For the next two hours, at agreed-upon times, we talked on Alpha, but he had no specific news from Magic. He only said that NATO was doing all it could to launch a rescue. Daybreak was coming. I prepared myself mentally to go back to my hole-up site. I would have to live with my disappointment and hope that the Bosnian Serbs hadn't picked up any of our communications. Then, around 4:15

A.M., Basher One-One came on Alpha with a glow in his voice.

"They're rounding up the boys right now," he said. "The assets are airborne. They're throwing everything they have at you. It's only a matter of time."

Yes, I cheered silently. For whatever reason, NATO had changed its mind. They were coming for me today—right now! I uttered a brief prayer to God and quickly found a hiding place behind a nearby dirt mound. This was hardly a hole-up site, but I could keep low for a couple of hours. Turning on the radio, I accidentally knocked off the volume knob. The knob, which also controlled the on-off function, had been loose since I had first used the radio six days ago, but now was no time to have a problem. In the darkness I spent the next ten minutes combing the grass before I found it.

In my last communication with Basher One-One, he told me he had to return to Aviano, but another pilot, Rock Four-One, would take his place and be my eyes and ears in the sky until I was rescued. Basher One-One signed off, and his replacement came on my radio within minutes. Unlike the voice of Basher One-One, I recognized the voice of Rock Four-One. It belonged to Captain Vaughn Littlejohn, a friend of mine who was calm, confident, and steady as a rock—just as steady as Tom Hanford.

"Conserve that battery power," Littlejohn told me.

"And be ready. We're here for you, we're going to get you out."

At 5:45 A.M., Littlejohn came back on the radio to say the rescue craft would be over my position in ten or fifteen minutes.

I kept looking around. Dawn was breaking. I could hear cows lowing in the distance and the infernal racket of the herders' bells, but I saw nobody. Just in case, I had slipped a bullet into the chamber of my Beretta. Before, I had been sure I would never use the handgun. Now, I was just as certain that nobody was going to stop me from leaving.

As I waited, I began to realize that the clearing I'd chosen for the helicopter landing was small, maybe too small to handle a good-sized ship. Maybe a chopper could hover overhead and drop me a safety line. I wasn't about to go searching for another spot, not in daylight, not with all the cows and their handlers due to be grazing in open fields. I scooted behind my mound of dirt and asked God to make the time go a little faster.

It was decided that the U.S. Marines on the *Kearsarge* were the best unit to make a rescue attempt. Stationed just miles off the Croatian coast, the U.S. Marines, once they were airborne in choppers, could reach me in less than forty-five minutes. The TRAP unit was one of the

U.S. Marines' best trained, and the unit was experienced in handling dangerous situations from Beirut to Haiti to the Persian Gulf. As long as NATO provided backup air support, the TRAP commander, Colonel Martin Berndt, had already told Vicenza, his men weren't afraid of a daylight mission. The U.S. Marines thought that I'd been in danger long enough, and they wanted to get me out as soon as possible.

At 4:39 A.M., the forty-two members of the TRAP force hit the decks of the *Kearsarge* running. The team was made up of expert riflemen, field scouts familiar with the Bosnian countryside, electronic warfare specialists, medics in case someone got wounded, and a translator in case communication with the enemy became necessary. Team members prepared for their mission by test firing their M-16s, painting one another's faces with camouflage paste, and receiving a last-minute briefing from their commanding officers. By 5:05 A.M., one minute before sunrise, they were in their two Super Stallion helicopters. Two Cobra assault helicopters with lots of firepower would escort the larger helicopters with the rescue team. The four choppers lifted off the deck of the *Kearsarge* and waited for their NATO air support to come on-line from air bases in Italy.

The NATO fleet that joined the U.S. Marines was like the air force of a small country: F-16 and F-15 fighters;

British Harrier jump jets, the kind that can take off vertically and just hang in the air; tank-killing A-10 Warthogs; F/A-18 Marine Hornets with special missiles to take out SAM batteries; and EF-111 Aardvarks and EA-6 Prowlers with the electronics to jam hostile radar. Eight flying tankers were sent up to meet all refueling needs. In addition, a set of planes and helicopters would wait, hovering off the Croatian coast, to provide any necessary backup assistance. NATO was taking no chances.

It took more than half an hour to assemble all the aircraft, and at around 5:45 A.M., the fleet headed toward the Croatian coast. The Hornets would streak toward me first, flying directly over my site to verify my coordinates. The Cobra choppers would follow, leading the actual rescue, with the two Harriers overhead to supply close air support.

Once the air fleet was feet dry, they began skimming over the hills and farms and forests, staying low and using fogbanks for cover. They were followed by the TRAP force in the two Super Stallions. The Cobras were only ten miles from my position and closing in fast. The job of the pilots of the Aardvarks and Prowlers was to pick up, jam, and, if necessary, destroy any Bosnian and Krajanian Serb radar activity. From intel they knew the location of the SAMs, and they waited to see if anyone would be spiked as I'd been six days earlier. The rescue mission was meant to be as secret as possible. No one was going to open fire unless put in harm's way. The next move would be up to the Serbs.

From my hiding place near the clearing, I watched the clouds begin to break up, showing a clear patch of blue. The ground fog had mostly peeled away, but some fog still hovered in the field below. I was on the edge of the mist . . . shrouded from anyone approaching by foot, but visible to my rescuers. I couldn't have asked for better weather conditions. Suddenly, I heard the welcome roar of a pair of F/A-18 Hornets overhead. It was a little after 6:00 A.M. One of the U.S. Marine pilots radioed and asked me to give him a mark. I let him know exactly where I was. His jet streaked off, but not before he promised that the rescue choppers would be there within thirty minutes.

That half hour was one of the longest of my life. In my head I went over the search-and-rescue procedure fifty times. I could have recited it in my sleep. When I finally heard the sound of helicopter blades beating the air, I jumped into the clearing. Trying to control myself, I called in to my radio to tell the pilots my exact position in relation to the Cobras. I could see the Cobra attack helicopters through a hole in the mist, but I didn't know if they could see me. The pilot of the first chopper radioed for me to "pop smoke."

I was ready with my flares and pulled the cap off the first one. Its red phosphorus smoke spiraled up through the fog, marking my position. Within twenty seconds, by the time the flare had faded, I could see the first Cobra directly overhead.

"We see you!" the pilot confirmed over my radio.

The floppy orange hat that I had wanted to throw away because I couldn't imagine a use for it was now on top of my head. I wanted to make myself as visible as possible. I popped a second flare, just in case, and waited for one of the Cobras to land or someone inside to toss me a safety line.

But the Cobras remained hovering in the air. It took me a few seconds to realize that they were only the advance ships. Their job was to make sure it was safe for the Super Stallions to land. One of the Cobras dropped some yellow smoke on a field about 200 yards to the south. Suddenly, two huge Super Stallions came into view behind a forest of trees. I watched them land just to the south of me. One of the Cobra pilots radioed and ordered me to run toward the Stallions.

Pistol in my right hand and radio in my left, I began zigzagging through the woods. My survival vest was flopping with my used flares and my compass. Just before I reached the field where the idling Stallions stood ready, I tripped and sprawled onto all fours. The Cobra pilot, still on my frequency, urged me to keep running.

"I'm going," I said as I picked myself up, "as fast as I can."

Breaking through the tree line, I found the two Stallions parked on a sloping, rock-strewn field. The area was filled with tree and brush stumps—hardly the perfect landing zone. The two Cobras floated above us, guns at the ready for any hostile encounter. And above the Cobras were the pair of Harrier jump jets. I didn't see any Bosnian Serbs, but if they showed up, I felt I was on the side of superior firepower.

U.S. Marines had jumped out of one of the Stallions and fanned out across the hilltop to form a defense perimeter. Either standing or kneeling, they had their M-16s pointed in all directions. I knew they were waiting on me, but for a few moments I just stood there. I didn't know which helicopter I was supposed to board. It was a strange feeling as I looked around and waited for someone to give me permission to move forward. After six long days of waiting, these last few moments were the longest yet. Finally, a burly young sergeant standing outside the gunner's hatch of the closest chopper began waving me in.

I ducked my head, fearful of the Stallion's rotor blades, and made a beeline for the open door. I had my Beretta waving in my hand, thinking I might still have to use it if the Serbs surprised us. To make sure the Beretta didn't accidentally go off, the sergeant kindly hit my wrist before I entered the chopper. The gun dropped to the ground and the sergeant picked it up for me. My floppy orange hat flew off my head, a souvenir I'd gladly leave for the Serbs. I no longer needed it.

We waited another minute for everyone to reboard the helicopters. I was shivering badly. Colonel Berndt slipped his jacket over me, and I was asked if I wanted to see a medic. I shook my head, but I took someone's canteen and polished off a quart of water in record time. Someone else served me a prepackaged meal of cold chicken stew. I couldn't believe all the attention I was getting, the number of men and aircraft that had been sent to rescue me. When I looked into the faces of the thirty U.S. Marines surrounding me, I was struck by how young they were— their average age, I would learn later, was nineteen. They had done their job with precision and perfection; I felt incredibly proud of them. More than that, I owed them my life.

At 6:48 A.M., six minutes after the two Super Stallions had landed, they lifted off the rock-strewn field and soared over a ridgeline, heading west to the Adriatic. I knew we were still not out of danger. A sergeant next to me said something about "taking fire," and I said yes, I'd taken fire in the last six days. It was so loud in the chopper that I hadn't heard him clearly. What the sergeant was really saying was that the *helicopter* was taking fire, *now.*

As the ground fog burned off and the Super Stallion glided over the Croatian landscape, Krajanian Serb antiaircraft artillery had opened up like the Fourth of July. Maybe their radar had picked up the Stallions coming over, and now that I was on board and there was no fog to hide us, they wanted badly to shoot us down. At seventy feet in length and able to travel at only 200 miles per hour, the Stallion was a fat and juicy target.

One round tore through our main rotor, while a second damaged the tail blade. A third punctured the cabin and, on the rebound, ended up meshed in a sergeant's canteen. Then, as if from out of nowhere, came the corkscrew white plumes of shoulder-launched SAMs. At least two or three were fired—and one passed just below us.

Please, God, I prayed, *let none of these good men get hurt. Let us all make it home again.*

Our door gunner returned Serbian fire. Others sat silently and grimly. Trying to evade the enemy, the pilot took the Stallion low to the ground, once more skimming over barn and house roofs. After five minutes, the antiaircraft fire came to an abrupt halt. At 7:15 A.M., we were clear of Bosnian airspace.

Relieved smiles and sighs broke out in the cabin. No one had been hurt. The Stallion, despite damage from the antiartillery guns, was on course for the USS *Kearsarge,* while the calm, blue waters of the Adriatic sparkled below. *That* was one of the most beautiful sights in the world.

TEN

By the time Basher One-One had made contact with me in the wee hours of Thursday morning, it was still Wednesday evening in the States. Everyone in the O'Grady household in Alexandria, Virginia, and my mom and her husband, Joe, in Seattle, Washington, were dazed and tired. My dad had shed eighteen pounds in the last five days, and Stacy and Paul didn't know what to say to him, or to each other, anymore. Hopes had been raised and then dashed too many times. When talking, they stubbornly refused to refer to me in the past tense, but secretly each was trying to adjust to the fact that I might be dead. This waiting couldn't go on forever. They had to continue with their everyday lives. Dad had his medical practice. Paul was due to start a job in North Carolina. Stacy was through with teaching for the summer, but she wanted to be with our mom in Seattle. That evening the three played a game of Parcheesi and had dinner, and Paul and Stacy turned in for the night. My dad, who was getting used to a sleepless routine, drifted up to bed and stared at the walls.

In Seattle, my mother spent Wednesday evening much the way she had the previous four nights, waiting for news of her son and trying to hold on to whatever hope she could. She had gotten into the habit of opening a world atlas to the page of the former Yugoslavia—now Bosnia and Croatia and Serbia—and running her finger over the page, over the roads and rivers and tiny towns. She thought of all the people who lived there. Maybe someone would be there to help her son. My mom basically believed in the goodness of people. Not everybody in Bosnia was the enemy. She would imagine I was somewhere on that page, among decent people, and the thought comforted her. But nights were hard. She didn't like to go to sleep. She felt she was somehow abandoning me if she took a break and went to bed, as if I were a sick kid who might need her for something.

At 12:48 A.M., Thursday morning, Eastern Time, the phone rang on my father's bedside table. He suspected it was his brother with another rumor about my whereabouts in Bosnia. The caller identified himself as Colonel Wald, my wing commander of the Thirty-first Fighter Wing, who had been in touch with my family since the shootdown. Tonight, Colonel Wald said, he had a different kind of news. Good news. Unbelievable news. He told my dad that I had been found, apparently safe and sound, and at this very moment I was being picked up by a rescue team.

Screaming that I was alive, Dad ran into Stacy's room and woke her with the joyous news, and then they both barged into Paul's room and began jumping up and down on his bed like a couple of kids. It was like Christmas and V-J Day rolled into one.

My mother and Joe got their phone call around 10:00 P.M. Wednesday night, Pacific Time, with the same news from Colonel Wald. My mom collapsed on the floor and sobbed wildly. It was as if, she said later, she had been holding everything in for so long, and now she just fell apart.

Like me, she would need a little time to readjust to a normal routine.

ELEVEN

As the Super Stallions approached and hovered over the deck of the USS *Kearsarge*, ready to land, it didn't seem as if my adventure could really be over. It was 7:29 A.M., the eighth of June. After six days of danger, fear, and desperation, of testing myself and my faith, I was back home. After the giant helicopters set down, I walked into a crowded sea of smiling faces and clicking cameras. The whole scene was very unreal. I pushed ahead through the throng of admirers and touched a few of the hands that eagerly stretched out to me. I listened to their congratulations and realized that these people considered me a hero.

The thought amazed me. I was a survivor, a U.S. Air Force officer who had done his duty under somewhat extreme conditions, and I had returned with honor. I had done exactly what I was supposed to do. Never once during my ordeal did I consider my efforts to stay alive and avoid capture heroic. I had simply used my wits and my skills to survive. In my eyes, after "T.O." Hanford and his wingman, the real heroes of the day were the sixty-one U.S. Marines on the four helicopters who had braved daylight, uncertainty, and the Serbs' heavy artillery to pluck one man out of the wilderness. The same was true for everyone connected with the rescue effort. They were all heroes because, in my book, a hero is someone who does something to help somebody else.

Once I was through the crowd of well-wishers, I turned over my tired and battered body to a team of U.S. Navy doctors. They scrubbed me down and started poking and probing me with needles. That included hooking me up to an IV to get fluids into my body and giving me a shot in each thigh to stop any infection from parasites. My temperature, I learned, had dropped to 95.2 degrees Fahrenheit, so doctors laid a large rubber heating blanket over me.

The doctors told me I also had second-degree burns on my cheeks and neck but fortunately no infection there. There were multiple scrapes and bruises on my hands and knees. I had mild dehydration as well as hypothermia and an elevated blood pressure and pulse rate. My most serious problem was a case of trench foot. This was a swelling of the feet caused by extended exposure to cold, damp, and frost. But with rest and warmth, I was told, my health would return to normal. Considering the stress of the six days, doctors pronounced me in pretty decent shape, if a little underweight. After eating only grass, leaves, and ants for six days, I'd shed twenty-five pounds. The Scott O'Grady Escape and Evasion Diet had been a resounding success, but I didn't think I could recommend it to friends.

I felt starved now, but the doctors didn't want me to eat until I finished with my IVs. I put on a bathrobe and, around 5:00 P.M., was visited by the U.S. Marines' intel officers. The wanted to debrief me—evaluate the entire rescue effort and find out if I'd observed anything about the Serb army. As I told them everything I knew, I realized how clever the Bosnian Serbs had been. In the year and a half before I was shot down, the cap routes of NATO aircraft had become very predictable. Because we were flying in the same place almost all the time, the Serbs had taken a chance and launched their missiles blind, without radar, at Wilbur and me. My F-16's normal radar-jamming abilities had nothing to jam. Only when the missile had come within seconds of my plane had the Serbs finally activated their radar. By then, as the missile came right at me through the clouds below, it was too late for me to do anything.

After a long, hot shower, I received a parade of visitors: the pilots and the men who had risked their lives to bring me back; my wing and squadron commanders, who flew in from Aviano; and the unsung heroes on the *Kearsarge* who had assisted with the rescue effort. Many brought gifts. One was a shoulder patch of Snoopy, the comic-strip character, in his World War I flying outfit complete with his famous scarf. Below Snoopy were the words BE

119

HUMBLE. The patch was normally given to sailors and marines who had rescued downed crew. I was receiving it because, technically, I had rescued myself, walking onto the Super Stallion without any assistance. I didn't think I deserved the patch—it was I who should be giving the sailors and marines gifts—but in the end it was the message that proved irresistible. When the chaplain finally came to visit, I prayed with him, and then I wept. I had truly been humbled during my ordeal; it was God who had kept me alive the last six days.

At 8:30 that evening, I was told that I had a phone call in the captain's quarters. In my robe and slippers I shuffled upstairs to the private cabin, eager to speak with my family. After my faith in God, and my belief in my fellow pilots and the forces of NATO, it was my love for my family, and their love for me, that had inspired me to survive. I picked up the phone, wondering if it was my mom or dad I would speak to first.

It was neither. The voice on the other end belonged to President Bill Clinton. I was in shock. We exchanged greetings, and then President Clinton said, "The country was on pins and needles, but you knew what you were doing. The whole country is elated."

"Mr. President," I replied, "I just want to say one thing: the United States is the greatest country in the world. God bless America."

"Amen," the president said.

Then it was time to call my family, first my dad's home in Virginia, then my mom in Seattle. My tears flowed freely as I spoke to Dad, Paul, and Stacy. I remembered how, pinned to the ground in some miserable hole-up site, I had been afraid I would never hear their voices again. Now the floodgates opened. For the next ten minutes everyone talked so excitedly it was hard to hear each other. Dad had already received a call from President Clinton, and as exciting and unexpected as that was, he, Stacy, and Paul liked hearing my voice even better. In a matter of hours the news media would be outside my dad's house. The members of the O'Grady family were about to become overnight celebrities, but for these few moments we cherished our privacy.

Speaking with my mom was just as emotional as hearing from Dad, Stacy, and Paul. My mom told me she had never given up believing that I was alive, but now she wanted to know how I was feeling. I told her I was in good shape physically and mentally, and that made her feel better. Finally, I went back to my ship's quarters, where I was served a glorious meal of crab legs and strawberry ice cream. I thought I would sleep like a log afterward, but all the excitement kept me on edge. I don't think I slept for more than four hours. When I woke, for an instant I thought that I was back in my apartment in Montereale Val Cellina, Italy, and that the last six days had been one big, bad nightmare.

A U.S. Navy corpsman brought me a breakfast of French toast, and after more medical tests, I had another debriefing with intel officers. I also met with Leighton Smith, the U.S. Navy admiral responsible for organizing the rescue effort, and we reviewed how the whole process had come together in such a short time. After lunch and a tour of the ship, it was time to say goodbye to everyone on the *Kearsarge.* I was still walking stiffly, feeling every sore muscle, but my spirits were as high as an F-16 can fly. Waving to everyone on the flight deck, I boarded the Super Stallion with my commander, a doctor, and several other Air Force officers, for a quick jaunt to the Italian coast. There we would pick up a Learjet for our leg back to Aviano. Finally, I thought, my life could return to normal.

I was very wrong. My life would never return to anything near normal. Aboard the Learjet I was warned to expect a gathering of friends at Aviano. When I stepped off the plane, a crowd of 500 was standing in a large hangar to greet me. Pilots, wives, officers, enlisted men, children—it was an overwhelming spectacle. I wasn't sure what I should do or say except wave back. I was led quickly to a car and whisked away to a private reception in a squadron building. Waiting for me there were Wilbur and "T.O." Wilbur was the first one I hugged. Then

"T.O." came up and told me that he had been Basher One-One. I was overwhelmed. I let him know that hearing his voice that night was a gift from God. His determination to find me and his ability to keep me calm were a debt I could never repay, I said. As good friends as we had been before my adventure in Bosnia, "T.O." and I were now bonded for life.

After the private reception I returned to the hangar full of my friends and their families. To honor my return, there was a flyover of sixteen NATO planes representing all different types of aircraft. Turning back to the crowd, I shook a bunch of hands, and a microphone was shoved in front of me. I had never been one for public speaking. Growing up, I was hardly shy about taking risks, and I was good at dealing with people one to one, but crowds brought out almost a shyness in me. I told myself to keep my speech brief, just as I'd done with my fellow Juvats in South Korea.

"The first thing I want to do," I said, "is to thank God. If it wasn't for God's love, and my love for God, I wouldn't have gotten through it. He's the one that delivered me here, and I know that in my heart.

"I also want to thank the United Nations, the United States, all the NATO countries. When I was out there, I knew you were all behind me—I could hear you, and I knew it. . . ."

I said some more thank-yous, received a long ovation, and rejoined my squadron mates and their families for a few quiet moments at the Triple Nickel snack bar.

Minutes later I said my goodbyes and left the squadron building, returning to my apartment for the first time since that morning. I'd left without having my breakfast. To step into my own shower, to throw my feet up on the sofa, to sleep in my own bed . . . there was nothing more comforting than being back home.

The following morning I felt anxious again. There was a major media luncheon, to be held at the officers' and enlisted men's clubs at Aviano. I was to be the big speaker. But I didn't have anything terribly new to say. And I didn't have permission from my commanding officers to talk freely about my six days, not until I was fully debriefed. As I walked into the room, I stared at more than a hundred reporters who represented newspapers, radio, and television stations around the world. Sitting next to "T.O.", Wilbur, and Colonel Wald, we were all surprised when the U.S. Air Force public affairs office began playing a tape of the emotional interchange between Tom Hanford and me, when we had first made contact on that lonely night and he had found me. It was the first time I had heard the tape. Hanford's voice was clear and determined, while mine sounded frail and tired. Listening to everything, I began to cry, and tried to hide my face behind a napkin. "T.O." started to get teary as well. I know some of the press joined us.

Suddenly "T.O." turned to me and said, "You big jerk, you made me cry on national television." I began to laugh, and so did "T.O.," breaking the tension. But when I went to address the reporters, most of them were still choked up, and a full minute passed before anyone had the composure to ask me a question. When the questions did come, it amazed me how much interest my adventure had created in the outside world. And from the questions I was getting, I could see that everyone considered me a hero, no matter what I said to tell them I wasn't. When I thought back on my life, I had never really had any heroes—except one. It was a pretty big exception. The person who had most encouraged me, stood by me, sacrificed for me, and taught me the importance of self-reliance was my dad. I thought I was the most fortunate kid in the world. And he would always be my hero. Just to keep things in perspective, remember who the real heroes are, I told myself as I finished answering everybody's questions.

By the end of the day I was feeling almost numb from all the attention. But at least it was over, I thought. I had no idea that, except for my family and relatives, anyone back in the United States really cared about what I had been through.

I flew home the next day on an Air Force C-20, accompanied by several high-ranking officers, including a colonel in public affairs who would help me with a few media engagements that had been lined up. When we landed at Andrews Air Force Base in Maryland and filed off the plane, I was totally taken by surprise. One of my first sights was a banner held high in the air, and I didn't even know who had made it.

BASHER 52
AMERICA'S BEEN PRAYING
WELCOME HOME
SCOTT O'GRADY

My throat knotted, and it didn't loosen any when a military band began to play, or a quartet of F-16s roared overhead to salute my homecoming. I met and chatted with General Ronald Fogelman, the chief of staff of the Air Force, and right behind the general, standing on the tarmac, was most of my family: my mom, my dad, my grandparents, and my brother and sister. I hugged Stacy the longest, so hard that I thought we might topple over. When she finally pulled away, it was to ask me if I'd remembered to wear the special cross she'd given me as a present years ago. I might have forgotten other things on that flight, like my St. Christopher medal and my flight jacket, but not her cross, I assured Stacy. I never took it off no matter where I went. She laughed with relief. That was how she knew, she said, I would come back alive.

That night, exhausted, I stayed in a downtown hotel and caught up on badly needed sleep. My family and friends partied at a local country club, toasting me and my adventure until the wee hours. I was sorry I couldn't be there, but I knew tomorrow was not going to be just another day in the life of Scott O'Grady. I wanted to be at my best.

My whole family and I were invited for lunch at the most recognized address in the United States of America: 1600 Pennsylvania Avenue.

TWELVE

Like a small, determined invasion, seventeen O'Grady relatives and friends descended on the White House the next morning. Hillary Clinton greeted us and made us feel right at home, particularly my seventy-nine-year-old grandmother, who insisted on telling the First Lady all about my seven-year-old cousin, Zack, and what a great fan he was of the president. While a staff member took my family on a White House tour, I met privately with President Bill Clinton and Vice President Al Gore in the Oval Office. The idea of sitting in the same famous room where our presidents had entertained important dignitaries and heads of states for almost two centuries was almost overwhelming. I remembered all the cross-country trips I'd taken with my dad, the many historical sites we'd visited, including the White House. I'd never dreamed that one day I would be honored in the Oval Office by the president of the United States.

I felt humbled, and might well have been speechless if my hosts hadn't been so relaxed and down to earth. I gave the president the squadron patch of the Triple Nickel, to add to his collection of mementos from other visitors more important than I. We talked for an hour about my experience in Bosnia while he assured me of what I already knew, that he and the people of the United States had not for one minute forgotten me in their thoughts and prayers. Thanking the president, I don't think I'd ever felt more proud to be an American.

After our Oval Office visit, the president himself led me on a tour of the White House. I was impressed by his knowledge of the history of various rooms and their furniture, especially those with military significance. One rather plain desk had been used for the signing of every U.S. treaty since the Revolutionary War. I stopped to admire it for what it symbolized. Each of our country's wars, to one degree or another, had been fought over the ideals of political freedom and individual liberties. While alone on the ground in Bosnia, I knew what it felt like to have no freedom and no rights. I would never take those ideals for granted.

A delicious lunch of mixed greens and crabmeat salad, grilled vegetables, and lamb chops was served in a private upstairs dining room. I told the president I hoped he didn't mind if I passed up my salad. Amid laughter, the president understood that after having to force myself to eat leaves and grass in Bosnia, my appetite for things green had not fully recovered. As we all ate, I listened to the day-to-day stories of the president and vice president. I saw that the job of running our country was the most difficult imaginable—even more difficult than trying to evade a hostile army for six days. I also thought that President Clinton was doing that job with sincerity and integrity. I was proud to call him my commander in chief.

After lunch it started to rain. The president and I jumped into his official limousine and were whisked off to attend a ceremony at the Pentagon. The event had already been scheduled for outside, so an honor guard hoisted umbrellas over each speaker as he gave his speech. The chairman of the Joint Chiefs of Staff, the secretary of defense, and finally the president addressed the crowd of high-ranking military officers and enlisted personnel. They described how my rescue symbolized a nation's commitment to the individual men and women who served our country and our allies.

When it was my turn to speak, my words, as usual, were brief and from the heart. They, too, addressed the theme of commitment to the individual, but with a particular emphasis.

"If you'll allow me to accept all of this fanfare in the honor of those men and women who deserved it more but didn't get it," I said, "to those who suffered a lot more than I went through, to those who were POWs [prisoners of war], to those who gave the ultimate sacrifice, both in wartime and peacetime, for their countries. . . . If you could do that for me now, I accept all of this. . . ."

Loud applause tumbled down, given, I believed, not for me but for all those selfless men and women of whom

I spoke. Overcome with pride and emotion, I turned to the president and raised my fists high over my head, giving my commander in chief the official "snakes" salute of the Juvats.

As incredible as my day had been, I left the Pentagon ceremony feeling that I'd had enough attention. I wanted to unwind now and reflect privately on all that had happened. With a close friend and the public affairs colonel who had guided me through these last few days, I headed for my favorite place in Washington, D.C.: Arlington National Cemetery. Since joining the U.S. Air Force, I had visited Arlington's rolling grass hills with its endless rows of white crosses many times, but as with my visits to the Vietnam Memorial, on each occasion I was deeply moved. There was plenty of history here to inspire me, from the simple stones for the Civil War dead to the eternal flame marking the grave of John F. Kennedy. All these men and women had given their lives for their country.

But today my emotions were stirred more than usual. Looking at the thousands of crosses, I wondered how many of these brave people had suffered and sacrificed far more than I, yet never received the applause and attention that I had. Most had given their lives quietly, their bravery known only to themselves, their comrades, and their loved ones.

When I was trying to survive in Bosnia, I had felt

incredibly unlucky. My plane and I had been in the wrong place at the wrong time. But having survived and been rescued, I was suddenly in the right place at the right time. The Great American Celebrity Machine wanted to make me a hero. As I'd tried to explain to so many people, I wasn't really a hero, I was a survivor—but the label seemed to stick anyway. As my gaze swept over the hallowed hills of Arlington, I knew who our country's true heroes were.

My last stop in the vast cemetery grounds was the Tomb of the Unknown Soldier. Approaching the steps leading up to the Tomb and the Memorial Amphitheater behind it, I watched silently with the rest of the crowd as the lone honor guard marched back and forth in front of the large marble crypt. The sun reflected off his visor, and the only sounds you could hear were the click of his boots and his palm slapping against the butt of his rifle. Inside the crypt were the remains of four unknown servicemen, one for each major war that the United States had fought in the twentieth century: World War I, World War II, the Korean War, and the war in Vietnam.

Receiving special permission, I stepped over the chain to the tomb itself and knelt before the crypt. This tomb symbolized the ultimate sacrifice. Not only had these four individuals given their lives to protect the freedoms of generations unborn, they had given their identities. No one could mourn them personally; no one could give them a parade or make a speech about their lives. But in giving everything and asking nothing in return, theirs was the highest honor of all.

ABOUT THE AUTHORS

Captain Scott O'Grady has been stationed in Korea, Germany, and Italy during his military career. He continues to serve his country as an F-16 pilot in the U.S. Air Force Reserve. He is also the author of *Return with Honor,* the *New York Times* bestseller published by Doubleday Books.

Michael French is the prizewinning author of half a dozen novels for adults and young adults, several nonfiction books for young readers, and two feature screenplays. He lives in Santa Fe, New Mexico, with his wife, Patricia, and their two teenage children, Timothy and Alison.